Ironing John

JAMES LEITH

IRONING JOHN

THE ATLANTIC MONTHLY PRESS
NEW YORK

First published in Great Britain in 1995 by Doubleday, a division of Transworld
Publishers Ltd.
First Atlantic Monthly Press edition, February 1996

Published simultaneously in Canada
Printed in the United States of America

Library of Congress Cataloging-in-Publication Data

Leith, James
    Ironing John / James Leith.
       p.   cm.
    ISBN 0-87113-615-5
    I. Leith, James. 2. Househusbands—United States—Biography.
    I. Title.
HQ756.6.L45   1996   306.87—dc20   95-36095

Atlantic Monthly Press
841 Broadway
New York, NY 10003

10 9 8 7 6 5 4 3 2 1

For all my family, but most especially my wife,
without whom . . .

Forewarned

THE IRONING-BOARD AND THE IRON ARE KEPT IN A cupboard in the utility room. The ironing-board is a narrow table with a pointed end that folds flat for storage. It also folds flat for its own amusement when you least expect it; usually trapping two or more of your fingers within its hinged metal jaws. The ironing-board is a deck-chair with an attitude problem.

The utility room is not, in fact, big enough for anyone to set up the ironing-board in it, plug in the iron, and stand beside the board doing the ironing. This is partly because the location of the power point and the length of the flex ensure that before you reach the end of the garment on the board, the plug comes out of the wall.

Even if it were big enough, the ironing person would get lonely stuck out there, when the kitchen is where the action is. So anyone needing to do the ironing sets the board up in the doorway between kitchen and utility room, plugs the iron in under the telephone point in the kitchen, making the telephone easy to reach should it ring (which it will) and allowing the person doing the ironing to hear the radio (on the other side of the kitchen) or mediate between bickering children at the kitchen table which is, sadly, not quite within striking distance.

One drawback to this location for the ironing-board is that it is immediately over the spot where the Great Dane eats his three meals a day and where his constantly available four-gallon bowl of water awaits his pleasure. I could, of course, move it. This would cause the Great Dane a considerable amount of mental anguish, and the fact is that I only remember about the bowl as I stagger through from the utility room with the half-erect ironing-board. Once the board is securely in position, it seems reckless to risk its collapse in order to move the bowl. The position of the board also means that freshly ironed shirts may be hung over the backs of the chairs at the kitchen table without becoming more creased than they were to start with.

The iron, of variable temperature settings and full of water for its steam facility, rests comfortably at the right-hand end of the board on its little asbestos mat. It is of some importance to the person intending to iron something that while the operation is in progress the telephone should *not* ring because its flex will become entangled with that of the iron, leading to the iron being dislodged from its little asbestos mat and falling into the dog's bowl, causing an electrical short circuit of spectacular proportions, or simply onto the floor, where it will merely cause damage to the parquet with collateral damage in the form of scalds and first-degree burns to the legs of the person who answered the telephone. Secondly, no-one should wish to pass from the kitchen to the utility room because, should they attempt to do so, the results will be almost identical to those brought about by the telephone, with the added entertainment of the ironing-board collapsing into the bowl as well. Thirdly, the dog, whose back is two inches higher than the ironing-board, should not become thirsty.

To Iron a Silk Mondi Blouse

1) Turn it inside out.

2) Set the iron temperature somewhere below that at which silk first adheres to the face of the iron and then spontaneously combusts. This is not very high.

3) Use a damp cloth to iron through because steam irons only steam when they feel like it.

4) For sleeves use the sleeve board we do not have.

5) Keep the iron moving or it will find a way through. (The blouse, that is.)

6) After ironing one sleeve, iron the other, the cuff of which will be soaking wet through immersion in the dog's bowl. Then iron the first one again. Ditto. Repeat.

7) When finished, hang the blouse carefully on the kitchen chair. While you are doing this the dog will come along for a drink.

8) Imagine doing this for at least six items each week for the rest of your life.

9) When you have finished the drink required by 8), you will know why

'The Secret of Ironing is to Avoid It.'

SHIRLEY CONRAN

CHAPTER ONE
Real Life

'Actions to be taken in the event of finding your vessel
in a rising wind on a lee shore:
1) Never allow your ship to get into this position . . .'

ADMIRALTY STANDING ORDERS

IN THE LONG, HOT SUMMER OF 1976 I WAS AN OUT-
of-work actor, father of a toddler, married to an equally
out-of-work and extremely pregnant journalist, and we all
lived in the only one-up, one-down cottage in Surrey.

None of us had any money.

We are talking seriously broke, here. We are not reminiscing
about down-grading to Côtes du Rhone or being unsure
whether we could afford Mustique AND Gstaad that year.
What we are talking about is signing on, and our only hope
of income being the uncommissioned children's book that
the wife and mother was grinding out from the cupboard

under the stairs; between nappy changes, that is, and getting the dusting done.

That was the year of the allotment, of home-brewed beer and home-grown marijuana. The beer was, without doubt, the most disgusting muck in the history of intoxication (with the possible exception of Chinese rice wine), but the grass was rather good. The beer came in a kit from Boots, and I made ten gallons at a time in a cleanish dustbin. The trick was to get the malt onto the 4 pounds of granulated sugar at the bottom of the bin before one of the Siamese cats came by. I was distracted once, just at the point where I'd poured the sugar into the dry bin, and when I came back a small blue-point kitten was looking up at me from the pile of sugar with an expression of ineffable joy at having finally discovered the sort of cat litter it liked. My wife was out, it would have been criminal to waste the malt, and since the beer tasted like cat's piss anyway . . .

The ganja in the greenhouse, on the other hand, merely required constant evasion of the polite interest of our fellow allotment holders. 'It's a sort of geranium, but I'm blowed if I can get it to flower, but it seems healthy enough.' Healthy? The bloody thing was seven foot high, with a trunk two inches across and a proliferation of leaves that would have made the drug squad's eyes water.

We cured it with honey in the bottom of the Aga and kept it for special.

Right up to the time, that is, shortly after our second son was born, that we got blasted and Penny started hallucinating wildly and had to be talked down like a mad, blind airline pilot. Never touched it again after that, but our pot-head friends got the benefit of a seriously good crop.

Between growing dope and brewing beer-substitute, I only really had time to cultivate the allotment where we grew, with typical townie-beginners' luck, the most amazing strawberries and all the vegetables we could eat. That was the year my mother-in-law watched me plant out four rows of seedlings before she told me you couldn't transplant carrots.

I'd been wondering why the miserable old bastard in the next allotment had been looking so cheerful. He it was who raised such a laugh telling his cloth-capped *compadres* how he'd found me in the dark, on my hands and knees with a torch, trying to block up earthworm holes.

When friends came to dinner I sometimes did the cooking, and I had been known to wash-up and, on one never to be forgotten occasion, I put the laundry in the washing-machine. Afterwards she decided that the need for supervision of this activity meant it was safer to do it herself, since this course of action was less likely to result in pale-blue everything, five sizes too small. Apart from all this domestic action, I was busily engaged in trying to get my golf handicap down.

This activity was frowned upon on the grounds that golf cost money, but since the wife and mother spent six hours a day squirrelled away in the cupboard under the stairs, I figured it was better all round if I was out. That way she wouldn't be disturbed by constant pleas for help in the childcare department; or have me under her feet should she want to get out of the broom cupboard and wash the nappies prior to rustling up the lunch, which I would be quite looking forward to as I strode down the eighteenth planning a surreptitious and exorbitant pint of genuine beer before arriving home to ask if I could help at all.

I thought I was doing pretty well, as a matter of fact. I thought I was the picture of the caring, sharing husband that the sixties should have produced from all that peace and love. She thought so too; except for the golf.

It was at this time that John Berger, famous for writing and donating literary prizes to the Black Panthers or whoever, wrote a piece in the *Guardian* about a Mediterranean peasant whose poverty meant he had to send one of his only two cows to be slaughtered. His family needed the meat. Since the size of his share was determined by weight, he sent the pregnant one. This was as moving a piece of writing as I had at that time encountered, and I felt compelled to share

it with my wife. I even offered to take over the roasting of
the shoulder of lamb with garlic and rosemary (a gift from
her mother), while she sat down and enjoyed the article.

Did I mention she was extremely pregnant herself?

Ten minutes later I was married to a vegetarian.

My natural delight at getting a lot more of the lamb than
I had anticipated was slightly, but not much, marred by the
knowledge that the poor old thing would now have to cook
two meals, one carnivorous and one vegetarian, two or three
times a day from here on in. My admiration for her moral
fortitude was as great as my admiration for her increased
workload . . . I thought about it often as I teed off for the
second round of the day.

Throughout that long lovely summer, full of good jokes
like Peter Jay being appointed Ambassador to Washington
and somebody else being appointed Minister for Drought,
it never once crossed my mind (no, nor hers neither, though
by your smiling you seem to say so) that since she was at
least attempting to earn us all a crust with the adventures
of Trueman Sam (he talked to trees, I seem to remember,
which could account for her later becoming biographer of
the Prince of Wales) and William the Spider, and I was
doing sweet sod-all, the natural conclusion just *might* be
that she should get on with the books and I should become
a full-time Houseworm and ease her load. Not me. Not in
1976. Not bloody likely. And this wasn't just chauvinism
. . . well, it wasn't ONLY chauvinism.

I'd tried 'helping out', but my every instinct about every
task told me that I should do NOTHING on my own
initiative. I always asked. I could make pastry when I was
ten years old, but at thirty I knew that it was her department
and I should interrupt her work to find out the proportion
of fat to flour. Notwithstanding this, I might occasionally
force myself to act without instruction, but a wife and
mother, no matter how engrossed in the next Children's
Book of the Year, can hear the click of the lid of the nappy
bucket from the other side of the house, can remember to

the minute when the sterilizing solution went in, and can yell 'don't rinse those yet' without stopping typing.

GIVEN all this, wasn't it really simpler to stay on the golf course, out of harm's way?

Our eldest son was two and a half, and he knew who was responsible for his welfare, all right. Toddlers fall down, and this one fell down a lot, and sometimes when he fell down I was the nearest potential source of what I fondly imagined was parental comfort, kisses better and large hugs.

Forget it.

From the moment I picked him up, he struggled and kicked until I put him down. Then he would return to wherever he'd fallen over, lie down again, and resume his howling where he'd left off. The curtain came down on this pantomime only when his mother came out from under the stairs, or back from the shops or wherever, and SHE picked him up. Lest anyone think this was caused by a typical male lack of sympathy and macho posturing, let me point out that he behaved exactly the same way if either of his grandmothers got to him first, something that made my mother at least want to give him a more substantial cause for his howling.

It must have seemed to her like inherited rejection.

My mother was, for many years, one of South Africa's leading actresses, with her own theatrical company and an extremely successful career. Like so many middle-class South African children born after the war I was looked after by a large Zulu lady who doted on me and I on her, and until I was three I think I spoke Zulu more frequently and fluently than English. One evening when she was not due at the theatre my mother indicated that she was going to bath me and put me to bed. I screamed blue murder and made it clear that while I might, in a spirit of friendliness, permit her to bath me, only Emma was going to be allowed to put me to bed. From 1976 I looked back on her undoubted desire to strangle me with nothing but sympathy.

My children exhibited every stereotypical preconception

about male/female roles in a way that suggests a triumph of the genetic over the environmental.

Our second child, another son, was born in July, and Penny had to return to hospital within a week of his birth, and he was left with me. As long as I was the only game in town, he was fine; but the minute she returned to the domestic fold, I was history. Perhaps she was giving out 'a baby's place is with his mother' vibrations. Perhaps I was giving out 'a father's place is on the golf course' vibrations. Either way, events and attitudes seemed to reinforce my very passive belief that even if I wanted to, I couldn't really be expected to take on a domestic role in the face of tacit opposition from everyone including the small blue-point Siamese cat, who regarded any meal provided by me as being a bonus, which didn't count towards his daily calorific entitlement.

We all thought, my mother especially, that the fact that I could, and occasionally actually DID, change a nappy was proof positive that the sort of stuff Jill Tweedie was writing in the *Guardian* couldn't possibly refer to me. I mean we even had *The Female Eunuch*, but neither of us had read it, and from 1975 to 1977 the publishing sensation was Shirley Conran's *Superwoman* books, the very title of which stated quite explicitly who was responsible for domestic chores, and who, by implication, for golf (with maybe a little brewing on the side).

Jill Tweedie was referred to throughout this period in our lives as 'BANG!'. This was short for 'Bang! . . . Speaking of the oppression of women . . .' which in turn comes from the joke about the boring little man who knew nothing about anything except his hobby, which was collecting guns. As a result he feels excluded from conversations about anything else. He finally writes to an agony aunt who suggests that he find a way to introduce his subject, with which he will then be able to dazzle the company. At the very next cocktail party he weighs in with, 'BANG! . . . Speaking of guns . . .'

The trouble with Tweedie at this time was not that she

wrote about feminism, but that she wrote about little else. As the *Guardian*'s golden columnist, she could turn any subject into a denunciation of male attitudes and female exploitation.

While 'helping' with the lunch I found this irritating, and longed for what I saw as her humourless banging on to be replaced by the brilliant wit of the anonymous creator of 'Letters from a Faint-Hearted Feminist' in the same paper, which made us both laugh a lot. Imagine my chagrin when I was told who wrote the 'Letters'. Yeah, well, anyway. It just goes to show that if SHE could take the mickey out of feminism, there was no earthly reason why I should take it seriously, right?

Anyway, I was soon to be rescued from any possible contemplation of domestic responsibility by a contract with the National Theatre. This reinforced my male role by giving me a job and, thank God, an income. Bread was being won, and by me. Rehearsals, performances, out-of-town try-outs, all meant that even the 'helping' around the house ground to a halt, and the wife and mother shouldered her suburban burden on her own.

She never did sell the children's story she'd been working on, so a house and two small children would be a piece of cake; she'd easily fit them in between her regular column in *Private Eye*, contributions to the *Evening Standard* and *Evening News* and the beginnings of a television career. After all, I had a proper job.

What really got up my nose was that not only did she cope with all this with no sign of strain, but I doubt if a week went by when she didn't cope with the entire domestic load and earn more than I did in her spare time.

No, I don't know 'what spare time?' either.

Years, as they say, went over and things changed. My stint at the National Theatre was followed by a season in Northern Ireland and several all but invisible (would, in some cases, it were so!) film and television roles . . . all of which conspired to convince me, looking in the dressing-room mirror, that just possibly this was no occupation for a grown man, especially one with more children than job offers.

The clincher was the economics of the Northern Ireland job. Nine weeks away, as good a repertory salary as a non-TV name could get, and at the end of it, having paid for board and lodging and travel, I came home to the bosom of my family with a net profit of twenty quid.

It was at this point that I went back to school.

I persuaded the Government, who seemed delighted to get another out-of-work actor off the dole, to give me a grant to do a post-graduate business management course. Then I went to my sister and scrounged a place at her extremely successful cookery school where I was surrounded by bright and beautiful and almost entirely female teachers and pupils, all of them keen to explain to me how to separate eggs.

Apparently you are not supposed to put the brown eggs in one pile and the white in another.

The intention behind all this was that I had decided that the time had come to take on the role of a responsible husband and father and get a proper job. I was going to work in restaurant management, where I thought I might earn a living while still being sufficiently in front of an audience to show off.

I eventually got a job the horrors of which a mere book cannot contain, but the result of which was that from that time on, any boss who was gratuitously rude to me got my resignation. This is not a characteristic particularly desirable in those who wish to remain in employment and climb the slippery pole to career success.

Almost unnoticed by her self-obsessed husband at this time, the lady of the broom cupboard had continued to be a full-time wife and mother. By now the house was slightly larger, her mother was living with us, and to the column in *Private Eye* she had added a biography of the Princess of Wales, another of Margaret Thatcher, a new career as a television presenter, regular contributions to the *Evening Standard* and was still earning more than I was. When she was really under pressure, her mother took over childcare and domestic duties while I worked for a chain of pizza restaurants and didn't think about it.

By 1985 a third son was added to the list of the wife's achievements and we'd moved to a really seriously large house, beside which, in her own cottage, my mother-in-law was now resident. How we got to this in ten years from a four-flight walk-up the wrong end of Westbourne Grove is a story that will occupy a later chapter, involving, as it does, the Wodehousian machinations of both the tabloid newspapers and my father-in-law and Uncle Toby, of whom a great deal more later.

The house was sufficiently large, and with both of us working our time was short enough and our income was high enough, to consider getting 'some help around the place'. This role was chiefly occupied by a succession of bodies whose employment ensured that the wife and mother had to add supervision and staff relations, including psychological counselling, to all the other tasks for which she was clearly responsible. I had a restaurant to run, after all. This restaurant was at least ours, but its location in Battersea and ours in Surrey meant, for me, a lot of time away from home.

You know, lunches in other restaurants to suss out the competition, golf days with the accountants, squash with the bank manager, you've no idea.

Meanwhile, nanny/housekeepers and gardeners came and went, and biographies and television programmes paid for them, and if there was any income left over the restaurant's losses soon swallowed them up.

Things continued in this hand-to-mouth fashion for four years, two biographies, two television series, God knows how many home and garden helps and a daughter to add to the fun. By now we had two sons at boarding-school; one at a day school anything up to half an hour away depending on traffic, who required delivery and collection at 9 and 3.15 respectively; and a daughter going to nursery school from 9 to 12. We also had a 'lady wot does' who was going to do the cooking but who had first to be taught to cook (not by the cookery school graduate, naturally, but by the wife, mother, journalist, TV presenter, etc.), a gardener who was having a nervous breakdown because he thought any unseasonal weather was God's personal judgement on the work that he'd done in our garden; and Penny had become, if the phone calls and faxes from around the world were anything to go by, the country's leading authority on the marriage of the Prince and Princess of Wales.

It was all this that allowed me to pursue my restaurant proprietor activities while she flew to Manchester every week accompanied by our daughter, just as four years before she'd flown to Glasgow accompanied by our son. (Note to young fathers: if you are in any doubt about the benefits of breast feeding, consider which of you has the breasts.)

In 1990 we sold the restaurant in Battersea and, with two former partners from the pizza business, opened a new venture half a mile from our home: a bar/brasserie in a former pub that for the next two years set the record (IBM and EuroDisney excepted) for making money disappear. If the recession was a contracting universe, this place was a financial black hole. And I was responsible for it. Well, me AND Nigel Lawson. It took us no time at all to realize that since the gravy train, if not derailed entirely, was at least likely to remain shunted into a distant siding for the foreseeable future, the new business couldn't afford to pay its directors' expenses, let alone any sort of salary, so we all agreed that to keep the business going we'd take any paid employment we could get elsewhere.

Finding non-executive directorships and consulting work, as the catering industry followed the builders over the edge of the first precipice of the recession, was about as easy as getting a Tory Minister to accept responsibility for something and resign.

Well, hell, if you had a well-paid job, would you? 'Specially in a recession.

And then the first tiny quiverings of an idea seeped into my subconscious and started to whinge for attention.

The home helps and gardeners were long gone, through a mixture of disenchantment (on our part) and poverty (also on our part). Mostly poverty. The *folie de grandeur* that allows you to see yourself occupying such houses as *Country Life*'s property pages are made of, is the same sort of folly that gets other people to sign up with Gooda Walker at Lloyd's.

The biographer from the broom cupboard had a year (The Major Year) in which to complete a book on the present Prime Minister (it was to become a matter for speculation which would be out first, the man or the book); the heavenly mother-in-law was fully occupied in protecting her own cottage from the marauding hordes of Goths disguised as our two smallest children, and I was out of work.

'Tell you what,' I heard myself saying, 'you write the book, write the articles and do the telly AND I'LL DO THE REST!'

It had taken nearly twenty years, but this New Year's resolution, 1993, meant I had finally gone about with all sails set and found myself off a very rocky lee shore with the wind rising and gusting hurricane force twelve.

CHAPTER TWO

Recruitment Blues

'If You Pay Peanuts You Get Monkeys.'

RUPERT MURDOCH

ANY SORT OF JOB STARTS WITH THE SICKENING REALIZ-ation that you have probably bitten off far more than you can chew.

People do not generally rise to their level of incompetence, they are born at it and simply get better at making it look as if they know what they're doing, until they reach a position where their actions actually matter, at which point no amount of jargon and other obfuscation can conceal their total lack of ability. I mean, take any given Chancellor of the Exchequer, it doesn't matter which. (Please.)

The only known exception to this rule is people who have somehow acquired loads of money and a position among the great and the good. There is a point beyond which you become stick-proof. If you work for the Midland Bank and come up £30 short on the cash, you're in trouble. If you're chairman of Graspley's Bank and come up £300 million short on Third World debt, you are paid £346,000 to go away (as a sort of reward?) and appointed Chairman of the CBI, or the Clearing Banks Association, or both.

Needless to say the position of Houseworm to the family does not fall into this category.

A brief outline of the position, job title, areas of responsibility, remuneration and reporting structure follows.

JOB TITLE: HOUSEWORM

LOCATION

The principal place of work is extremely conveniently situated, and relocation expenses are not offered. The workplace is usually within motoring distance of local amenities, and successful applicants will be expected to provide their own transport for the benefit of the business. Successful applicants having existing areas of responsibility within the organization, such as horticulture, DIY, tax planning and financial management (or even occasional catering), will be expected to continue to carry out these duties in addition to those listed below.

(IT CANNOT BE TOO STRONGLY EMPHASIZED THAT WHILE EVERY ATTEMPT HAS BEEN MADE TO COVER THE PRINCIPAL DETAILS OF THIS POSITION THE LIST OF RESPONSIBILITIES CANNOT BE ASSUMED TO BE DEFINITIVE, AND THE SUCCESSFUL APPLICANT MUST BE PREPARED TO BROADEN THE HORIZONS OF HIS RESPONSIBILITY AT ANY TIME. ANY REDUCTION OF THE AREAS OF RESPONSIBILITY IS NOT PLANNED, AND, IN THE UNLIKELY EVENT THAT ANY SUCH REDUCTION SHOULD OCCUR, IT SHOULD BE REGARDED AS A JOKE, and a temporary joke at that.)

Job Description

The successful applicant will report to the Househead whose qualifications include wifehood, motherhood, right-on sisterhood, breadwinnerhood and several years' apprenticeship as Houseperson, a job similar to that of Houseworm, but with status and historical and social justification.

Areas of Responsibility (General)

In the case of the particular position on offer in this case, responsibilities include:

One House

Comprising 6 bed., 3 rec., 2 bath., kit., hall, liv.rm., playroom, study, gge. and toolshed. All subject to subsidence. The applicant will be entirely responsible for the general appearance and presentation of both interior and exterior aspects and for the implementation of the Househead's policies as determined by the Househead from day to day. Consistency will be highly regarded in the implementation of these policies, but the policies themselves may change from day to day or even hour to hour (*see* 'The Conservative Party, 1990–93').

One Garden

Comprising 12 acres inc. 2 paddocks, deciduous woodland, lawn, pool, small stream, veg. garden, chicken house, potting sheds, greenhouse and tractor shed. The applicant will be responsible for lawn and flower-bed maintenance, vegetable and fruit production, planting and propagation, pest suppression (this is *not* to include either the Househead's dog *or* children) and all tasks necessary for woodland husbandry and the provision of logs for fuel.

Personnel

The successful applicant will be responsible for the nutritional, pastoral and psychological welfare of the following:
the Househead, the Eldest Son (19), the Second Son (16),
the Third Son (8), the Daughter (5), the Dog, the Five
Cats, the Rabbit, the Guinea-Pig, the Six Chickens, the
Two Geese, the One Cockatiel and the Snail the Daughter
Brought Home From School Last Week.

He will also be required to provide tea and/or coffee
(usually with three sugars) for all plumbers, electricians,
washing-machine and telephone engineers, painters, decora-
tors, underpinners and delivery drivers who may from time
to time have occasion to call at the place of business. Also for
any of their friends, wives, girlfriends or offspring who may
be accompanying them. The provision of such refreshment
will not, in the view of the Househead, constitute proper
and sufficient reason for the Houseworm's normal duties
being behind schedule, notwithstanding that provision of
the said tea and/or coffee will have led to the Houseworm
being subjected to up to an hour of reminiscences on
one, some or all of the following topics: 'What I done
in the Warwuh', 'Kids These Days', 'The Contraflow on
the B3478' or 'You want to watch that flat roof guvnor
it's a bit iffy tell you what a mate of mine can do it for
you two hundred quid all in'.

Areas of Responsibility (Specific)

Catering

While early-morning tea duty may, from time to time,
alternate between the Househead and the Houseworm,
the pouring of said tea for both, as well as for any of
their children who have joined them in bed for the ritual
of 'THE FAMILY LIE-IN (pronounced Lion)', will be the
responsibility of the Houseworm, as will liability for all tea

spilt on the duvet, his dressing-gown or said children due to hangover, encumbrance by three or more cats or that damn silly teapot we should have got shot of years ago.

Breakfast will be sufficiently closely supervised by the Houseworm as to ensure that departures for school and/or television studios are not delayed by tardy preparation of toast or less-than-prompt cleaning of teeth.

Lunch will be provided at 1 p.m. for all those at home. Adolescent and post-adolescent children will be woken in sufficient time for them to have completed breakfast before starting lunch (say 12.50 p.m.). Lunch will consist of home-made soup or bread and cheese on no more than three occasions per week, and baked potatoes on no more than one occasion (*see* children's supper, below). The provision of tinned or frozen anything will be regarded as gross misconduct and could lead to summary dismissal (dream on). In any case, both younger children reserve the right to reject any dish out of hand. Such rejection will generally take the form of a single expletive, viz. '*Yuk!*'

In the event of such rejection the Houseworm will *not*, especially if observed by the Househead, either resort to physical violence or sulk. Lunch will be cleared away in sufficient time for the dog to be walked before the children need to be collected from school.

Homework will be supervised to the extent that suggestions, requests, pleas, instructions and orders to stop watching television and get on with it will be issued at a rate of not less than three per hour until supper, which it is pointless to serve until after *Neighbours*. At this point, the instructions will be varied to cover 'Eat your supper while it's hot and get your maths book out of the gravy', to which the conventional reply will be, 'Do you want me to do my homework or not?'

Children's supper should be wholesome and nourishing, not to say virtuous, irrespective of the fact that the daughter has, for eleven weeks, eaten nothing but pasta. The Houseworm, who knows better than to indulge this peculiar whim right off, will first prepare and serve a lentil dish accompanied by mashed potato and peas. Once he has established, from the frequency of the expletive noted above, that the daughter wishes this dish to go the same way as breakfast's shredded wheat, he will ensure that it is replaced, like this morning's cereal, by a microwaved plate of spaghetti and tomato sauce from the substantial bowl the wise Houseworm has available at all times. The Houseworm will never cook less than 1 kilo of pasta at a time.

Adults' supper will be served only when the small children have been bathed, got into their pyjamas, cleaned their teeth, been read to, had a game of Happy Families (at which the daughter cheats), got into bed, got out of bed, been kissed good night and put back into bed, got out of bed, been yelled at, got back into bed, got up to ask for a glass of water, spilled it, been bellowed at, burst into tears and been threatened with mutilation.

Supper will also only be served after the Househead has been poured a large glass of something and been listened to sympathetically re the horrors of make-up, wardrobe, production assistants and male, ego-dominated producers. Likewise national newspaper editors.

It is not anticipated that it will only be at this point that the Houseworm starts to think about what is going to be done about supper.

On the contrary, it is anticipated that once the glass has been poured and the horrors commenced upon, not more than 20 minutes will elapse before the service of at least two nourishing and politically correct vegetarian courses containing both fibre and protein. The eating of a surreptitiously acquired steak by the Houseworm while muttering imprecations against 'pale brown fart food' will be grounds for disciplinary action.

Household Tasks

a) Dusting (feather). The upper walls and ceilings will be

maintained in such a way as to avoid having the house offered a research grant by The Arachnid Society.

b) Dusting (cloth). The successful applicant will be expected to so apply himself that the Househead will not be able to write, using only her index finger, the words 'Kilroy was here, where the hell were you?' on the surface of the hall table. Well, not more than once a month, anyway.

c) Polishing. This will be expected to follow dusting (*see above*) and precede hoovering (*see below*).

d) Hoovering. The neglect of this task for a period exceeding 30 days shall be regarded as grounds for the Househead to become extremely sarcastic. She shall be entitled to remark that she could have sworn we had a vacuum cleaner once but perhaps she was mistaken, but who knows what could be concealed beneath the pile of December's ironing in what used to be the broom cupboard.

e) Clearing up. This task is frequently a prerequisite to the satisfactory performance of 'Hoovering' (*see above*), since omitting it can lead to the ingestion by your vacuum cleaner of pearl earstuds, monsters-in-my-pocket and small furry creatures brought in in a terminal or semi-terminal condition by one or all of the cats.

f) Laundry. This will be done on a daily basis for under-clothes and children's clothes, once every two or three days (depending on their hygiene coefficient) for adults' clothes, and once a week for sheets. If sheets need to be cracked to get them in the washing-machine they've either been left too long on the bed or the Houseworm's got a lot luckier and a lot more energy than is generally regarded as the norm.

Adolescents' socks (*see 'hygiene', below*) should be inciner-ated rather than washed provided (a) that the home furnace is fitted with one of the new sub-atomic, anti-pollution filters and (b) that you can catch them (the socks, that is).

Tumble-dryers are provided for all but the most impover-ished Houseworms, and should ensure that all that running back and forth to the washing-line in the pouring rain is a thing of the past, provided the following guideline is strictly adhered to: THE MORE EXPENSIVE AN ITEM OF CLOTHING IS THE LESS IT CAN BE TUMBLE-DRIED.

Retro-couture guru Jean Paul Armindamani designs the £200 T-shirt and you can't tumble-dry the bloody thing. What's more, you're supposed to IRON it. ('It's a T-shirt, for God's sake,' will not be deemed an appropriate response.)

g) Ironing. It is not acceptable for the Houseworm to point out that since Diana Spencer got married in a silk dress that she had clearly slept in the previous night, ironing is no longer necessary as a means to sartorial acceptance. While the Houseworm may conceal an unironed shirt beneath a sweater to carry out HIS duties, the Househead does not expect to address the CBI in a silk blouse that's simply been boil-washed and placed in the tumble-dryer on 'high'.

h) Shopping. The organized Houseworm will ensure that sufficient records are kept current and stocks held to guarantee that one shopping expedition per week is all that is necessary. Applicants are not taken on in order to spend their time swanning about in the family motor.

i) Sewing and mending. It is essential to the continued success of the consumer economy that nothing is ever mended. Articles in need of repair should be discarded in the appropriate recycling receptacle or Bosnian relief bin.

Sewing is permissible only so far as the activity relates exclusively to name tapes. Smart-arse Houseworms who save time and thread by sewing tapes on in a loop using one line of stitches through both ends of each tape will be disciplined. No Househead is prepared to have rival wives and mothers commenting on the slipshod ways of her family, and the specification for name tapes is that the cotton, to match either the garment or the tape, be stitched at a rate of not less than 30 stitches to the inch applied ALL ROUND THE TAPE. The fact that this policy, when applied to tapes fastened to the elasticated tops of socks, means the tape stitches break as soon as the sock is pulled on is an observation which the Househead is not prepared to dignify with a reply.

j) Hygiene.

1) Personal. The Houseworm is expected to be presentable at all times (within reason, buddy. A shower rate exceeding two per day and the sprinkling of aftershave in socks will lead to conversations, not to say full disciplinary hearings, about that blond bimbo at the school gates and a close monitoring exercise on the frequency of sheet changes).

2) Familial. i) The Househead's toilette is not within the Houseworm's area of responsibility. If she requires his opinion she will ask for it. ii) The eldest son's hair, while strictly speaking his own responsibility (all three feet of it), can be pointed out as being in need of shampoo only if tact is employed, since he is now two inches taller than the Houseworm, and although about three stone lighter, with him it's muscle. Sniffing loudly and ostentatiously in the immediate area of either of the elder sons will only lead to concerned enquiries about colds, flu and nasal congestion. Scientific enquiry has confirmed that adolescents are entirely without a sense of smell, and, if chastised, without a sense of humour. In the interests of health and safety (his own), the Houseworm is advised to inhale deeply immediately prior to entering any adolescent's room, and to hold his breath throughout the necessary physical contact and dumb show required to get them downstairs so they can have breakfast and run up the phone bill in the eleven minutes before lunch. iii) The Houseworm is entirely responsible for the hygiene, health and appearance of both children under ten. This involves more than running the bath and telling them to get in, wash, shampoo their hair, get out, clean their teeth, clean the bath and get into their pyjamas and their beds in that order without disturbing the Houseworm's involvement with the Playmate of the Month. iv) It is not anticipated that in the performance of his duties the

Houseworm will be subject to either The Health and Safety at Work Act or The Food Hygiene Regulations, although removing diesel oil or weedkiller from the hands before preparing supper is generally expected unless the children have been particularly trying, or the Houseworm is preparing dough or pastry, either of which are extremely effective hand cleaners and will remove most forms of grime up to and including engine oil.

PSYCHOLOGICAL PROFILE AND PERSONALITY OUTLINE

The successful applicant will be expected to deal on a day-to-day basis with non-company personnel with whom the Househead has established relationships from fleeting (a school-gate mother with whom, for thirty seconds, she had some gynaecological quirk in common) to permanent (like Uncle Toby, for instance). Likewise with the individuals, male and female, who comprise the social whirl of sons numbers one and two. Likewise with the parents of the 'best friends' of son three and daughter. 'Best friends' only ever occur one at a time, but their identities are subject to change without notice, or indeed any perceptible passage of time, and the Houseworm will be expected to keep up.

THE HOUSEWORM WILL ON NO ACCOUNT ATTEMPT TO EITHER ADVANCE OR RETARD ANY OF THE ABOVE RE-LATIONSHIPS. HIS IS A WATCHING AND HOLDING BRIEF, AND THE DEVELOPMENT OF SOCIAL OR FAMILIAL RE-LATIONSHIPS OTHER THAN HIS OWN IS STRICTLY OUTWITH HIS REMIT. SIMILARLY, ASSUMPTIONS MUST NEVER BE MADE THAT ANY GIVEN RELATIONSHIP IS AS IT WAS THE LAST TIME THE HOUSEWORM WAS PAYING ATTENTION.

In other words, and to summarize, the successful appli-cant will be conscientious and discreet, efficient and reticent, may hold opinions within reason but not within earshot, and must, above all, have the one quality that will identify him unerringly to those among whom he used to be one of the lads. He must, in the half-witted opinion of said lads, have become so wet you could shoot snipe off him.

I got the job.

CHAPTER THREE

My Animals and Other Family

'Life's a bitch and then you die.'

BETTE DAVIS

PERHAPS, AT THIS POINT, SOME SORT OF OVERVIEW OF 'life with the Leiths' might be useful in providing the reader with the full horrors of the task so sketchily set out in the previous chapter.

The day we acquired a house large enough to accommodate my expanding family AND my mother-in-law, she moved in.

All the Les Dawsons at the back can siddown.

Pamela Mary, a.k.a. La Belle Mere (the capitals are intentional), is the safety netting, the escape route or the emergency services upon which the happy functioning of our overlarge family depends.

As her husband, who lives near by, would be the first to acknowledge, we got the best out of her move.

Sir John Junor, unique among editors, columnists and fathers-in-law, provided her with the cottage which meant we could afford to buy our present house and set us out on the voyage through thick and thin that culminated in housewormery.

Pamela Mary Junor is the still, calm eye at the centre of the personality-hurricane that one meets in The Editor (the capitals are still intentional). The first time I met him, he took his darling daughter and her newly acquired boyfriend out to dinner in the second smartest restaurant the environs of St Andrews University could provide. There, by way of trial by alcohol, he generously filled and refilled my glass to the point where I became convinced that he wished me to fall down, preferably for ever.

I nobly resisted gravity until coffee, when, in handing him a cup, I inadvertently dropped the spoon.

He looked at me.

'Funny, isn't it,' he mused, 'how these things always happen after you've had a drink?'

A DRINK? JJ has never poured a guest *a* drink in his life. His natural generosity, coupled with an equally natural curiosity as to vino-induced *veritas*, leads him to put all his many guests through this sort of test. It is often based on his persuasive enthusiasm and elegiac descriptions of the charms of Calvados.

A long-time enthusiast for the Norman coast of France, he holidays every year in the fishing port of Barfleur, whither he was wont to sail in his 32-foot Bermuda sloop, *Outcast*, crewed by anyone (sons-in-law a speciality) stupid enough to volunteer.

He now owns a charming house in the town, but he and his family used to live on his boat while eating, golfing and socializing their way round the Cherbourg peninsula. This is

where he annually got hold of suspicious-looking unlabelled
bottles of Calva', bottled, to hear him tell it, by the light of
the full moon in some apple orchard outside St Vaast le
Hougue. This moonlight bottling was supposed to provide
extra potency or something, as if the stuff needed it.

To this day, one of my oldest friends, and best man at
my wedding, cannot hear the word 'Calvados' without
uttering an involuntary groan. He arrived two days before
the wedding in 1970, and was billeted upon JJ and Pam,
and during his first evening JJ was in his element. My friend,
like his host for the evening, is very Scottish, a member of
the Royal & Ancient Golf Club, and an enthusiast for single
malt whisky. I could feel the brake that the presence of an
uncultured South African was putting on their Caledonian
reminiscences, and furthermore I'd been through this sort
of evening before.

I took myself off to bed at the point where I still held out
some vague hope of being able to get into it, and left the
two of them to it.

At about 2 a.m. I was woken by my Scottish friend, who
had clearly been persuaded of the merits of Calvados on top
of Glenmorangie, and who was unable to either speak or
find the bed he had fallen over.

I've never seen JJ touch the stuff.

Anyway, it was largely due to The Editor that we acquired
a house considerably above our station.

It was also largely due to the *Star* newspaper, a tabloid
kind enough to serialize, for a substantial fee, the breadwinner's views on the personality, characteristics and marital
state of our future king. I think that the fee was substantial
enough to feature centrally among the reasons for the *Daily
Star*'s editor's subsequent move to pastures new.

La Belle Mere, secure in her own cottage where she
endures the ravages of time and our children with great
equanimity, lives a life spent reading or gardening depending on the season. The first sign of spring around here is
not, as elsewhere, the sight of sunlight playing prettily on

swathes of daffodils, although we get that, too; but rather the sight of Pam, arse-up in the herbaceous border, attacking weeds with a dedication that would procure her a job with any landscape gardener in the country.

The onset of winter, on the other hand, is marked by her retreat into her cottage and a pile of books that would make a Booker judge wince. Here she is frequently disturbed by our children, all of whom adore her, and all of whom, whenever the Houseworm even looks like turning, can be heard to say 'CANIGOTOPAM'S'OUSE' as the door slams behind them.

Sons numbers one and two retire to the peace and calm of her cottage in order to read, whenever it seems to them that their maturity may mislead the Houseworm into suggesting that they might HELP.

The smalls know that no matter how unwilling their father may be to indulge in a flour-and-water session on the kitchen table he has just cleaned and laid, Pam will be happy to oblige. It's like living next door to a saint and being constantly found wanting in the eyes of the congregation.

There are areas, however, where the humble Houseworm is the only game in town, and I very much wish that there weren't.

The same Murphy governs the laws of household management in large houses as in small, but the differences lie in the scale of the catastrophe. The first law states that no mechanical breakdown that requires the attendance of any sort of engineer will happen until after 5 p.m. on a Friday evening, generally when the following Monday is a bank holiday. Further, that when the mechanical breakdown DOES occur, it will select the only machine without which the Houseworm DEFINITELY cannot manage to get through the next twenty-four hours, let alone three days. Washing-machines, for example, will NEVER simply fail to fill, or not start.

What happens is this: the Houseworm carefully sorts the available laundry into piles that might, as it were, be marked

'URGENT', 'MOST URGENT' and 'BEGINNING TO
TAKE ON A LIFE OF ITS OWN'. Carefully avoiding
the last for fear of catching something, the Houseworm
then loads the 'MOST URGENT' pile, containing all the
children's school clothes for next week (we are planning a
weekend away), into the machine and sets it going.

Eleven minutes and thirty seconds later, with the cylinder
full of soapy, dirty water and a tangle of clobber, the machine
lets out a distressed series of unfamiliar beeps, and on its
nasty little green digitized face appears an 'error code' which
invariably decodes as 'call engineer'.

Not even uttering a high-pitched scream of rage, as I do,
and kicking it, as I also do, will allow me to get the clothes
out, because, miracle of modern science that it is, the door
won't open when it's got water in it.

At moments like this only La Belle Mere will do. She is
deputed to call the engineer's answer-phone and tell it that
she is Lady Junor, wife of the Flogger of Fleet Street, and
say that if he isn't round here in thirty seconds, his most
intimate secrets will be revealed in a tabloid exclusive.

Whether she does this or not, I don't know, but, by the
time we get back from our weekend away, the machine is
fixed, and all the laundry, including the 'LIFE OF ITS
OWN' pile, has been washed, dried, folded and placed in
the airing cupboard.

Did I say 'saint', or what?

What has been got out of the machine's filter by the
engineer, namely seven by now badly bent coins, two bits
of Lego, one monster-in-my-pocket and enough cat and dog
hair to knit a rug, has also been left for our inspection.

This is the engineer's doing. What does he want, for God's
sake, an apology?

Until you have been reprimanded by the man from
Hotpoint for not putting water-softener in the dishwasher,
nor washing down its interior walls with vinegar on a daily
basis as set out in the handbook provided, you have not
been exposed to any sense of either authority or discipline.

At least my commandant in the South African army just told me I was a 'blerry disgrace and probably a communist and get out of my office before I have you shot'.

This bloke manages to make me feel as if I've assaulted his only daughter and betrayed my country into the bargain.

Those of you thinking that it's only because of my mother-in-law that I can claim to have conquered the peaks of housewormery are probably right, but there are areas where not even La Belle Mere will venture, namely the sewers.

She doesn't do counselling, either. (Unless you count, 'Oh, don't be ridiculous, I've never heard such nonsense,' as counselling.)

The Major Year opened with a prelude, the horrors of which almost convinced me that from then on things could only get better. Between Christmas and New Year, having coped with the festivities with, I thought, some aplomb, I arrived home from the pub to be informed that we had something of a crisis on our hands, and our New Year weekend guests had turned up in the middle of this crisis and I had better do something about it on account of this is my department now, right? This, in fact, had always been my department. (*See* Job Description, under 'existing areas of responsibility'.)

The central heating wasn't working because the pump had seized (it was about minus two outside), the drains (for the second Christmas in a row) had backed up, and the nanny was in tears because her bloke, our gardening genius, in a fit of Yuletide remorse, had decided that he had to give up both his job and her, and get back to his wife and daughter on account 'he couldn't stand the aggro no more'.

The Househead person, trained Samaritan that she is, left her word-processor to take on a counselling session in Pam's cottage, where, suspiciously, the central heating was working very well at about 80 degrees, just how she likes it.

Our lady guest took on lunch, wearing two overcoats and a pair of gloves.

Her husband took on the laying of fires in every room that boasted a fireplace, and I set off down the garden with my large bundle of drain rods, a shovel, and the doohickey that is supposed to lift drain-covers but doesn't.

Now most houses sport a couple of drain-covers, complete with rodding eyes Dyno-Rod for the use of, but we are unlucky enough to have no less than five, at twenty-yard intervals down the garden, over a main drain that eventually empties (sometimes), into the council sewer that runs slap across the middle of the paddock. When THAT baby backs up, the holes in the industrial-sized drain-cover force out as picturesque a brown geyser as can be seen in these parts. It can usually be seen, and smelt, from as far away as Godalming. But when that happens, the Council come and fix it. With my own drains, I was on my own.

I shall spare the reader the more intimate details of the task that fell to me that New Year, except to say that all five drain traps were full, and when I cleared one the next remained backed up. Add to this the fact that the effluent surrounding said drain-covers provided the dog with every ingredient of his favourite stuff for rolling in, fox-droppings excepted. Why *do* dogs prefer rolling in fox-plop to rolling in the human equivalent? Search me, but it probably means something to the hunt saboteurs.

On this occasion, no fox having provided him with the necessary, Ballou was prepared to make do. He also thought that all those sticks I was pushing into holes in the ground formed the equipment for a game I wanted to play, in which he was required to growl, splash about, and try to pull them out again.

I got back to the house two hours later, in a state that made a bath a precondition of access to human intercourse.

During my absence, fires had been laid and lit in just about every room, and as a result of these particular chimneys having been swept approximately never, due to the wonders of central heating, the entire house was now full of smoke, all the windows were wide open (the temperature was still minus two) and our guests were all assembled on the lawn. Penny was still deeply committed to her infidelity counselling and I can't say I blame her.

All the children had taken themselves off to PAM'S'OUSE at the first sniff (literally) of trouble, and were happily ensconced in front of festive telly.

I took to my bath and a large Scotch and vowed that straight after the holiday I would have a second central heating pump fitted in parallel, just as my brother-in-law has always done in every house he's ever owned.

If there's one thing I can't stand it's a smart-arse.

CHAPTER FOUR

Household and Management

'If you want to be lazy you have to be efficient.'

SHIRLEY CONRAN

ON DAY ONE OF MY NEW CAREER I WAS UP BETIMES. WHAT the performance of my new job was going to demonstrate was the essential difference between men and women, the masculine, methodical and systematic operator as opposed to the intuitive, feminine, scattergun approach.

I'd read all those management handbooks with titles like *Prioritization and Time Management*, usually by some Californian whose idea of a tough job would be Chief Executive of IBM.

The facts are these: the CEO (notice I have the jargon and acronyms off pat) gets to work around 8 a.m. and has his secretary bring him a cup of coffee while he gets through only that part of his mail that only he can deal with. This does not take long.

He then holds meetings and reviews performance with those whose job it is to tell him good news, and then he has lunch with Bill Gates of Microsoft and tries to winkle out of him how he does it. His limo gets him back to the office in time to meet the international finance director who needs to discuss rescheduling their Chase Manhattan credit line (what's to discuss?) before the executive board meeting at which the forthcoming pro-am at Palm Beach tops the agenda.

That evening he addresses the annual dinner of the Securities and Exchange Commission Officers for a Republican America on the subject of 'Kickin' Ass and Makin' Money'. He arrives home pooped and wishes to know why his wife is in bed asleep instead of downstairs holding his slippers. This leads to replacement of said wife by a younger trophy model who is not only downstairs holding his slippers, but is prepared to hold his dick in her other hand.

This goes on for some years until finally a loss of six billion smackers means he can retire to Palm Beach on a pension of God knows what and sit as a non-exec on boards from Baltimore to Bangkok.

Real people, and nobody would INVENT a Houseworm, have schedules like this: 6.30 a.m. Get up, let dog out, clear up cat sick that dog has not already eaten, feed by now hungry cats, make tea, empty dishwasher, lay table for breakfast, collect school clothes from tumble-dryer and return to bed with tea until 7. Get up again, get children up for school, shave, shower, get children up again, find Househead's Mondi blouse which he should not have put in that drawer, find daughter's sock and son's homework and get downstairs to pour muesli and make coffee and toast.

(Cooked breakfast? Don't you KNOW about cholesterol?)

Feed chickens, put the rabbit and the guinea-pig in the outside run and check that the children have given them food and water. (Ha!) Herd the troops upstairs to clean teeth, get the car out, load up satchels, monsters-in-my-pocket and snail in a jam jar and leave for school only after making sure the dog can't get out.

By this time the CEO is just saying, 'Do you have my coffee, Janice?'

9.00 a.m. Return from school to be faced with such break-fast detritus as the dog has seen fit to leave uneaten. Since the dog is a Great Dane, and, being a petite specimen of the species, only marginally smaller than a Shetland pony, this does not include anything that was left on the table in the kitchen, whether or not encased in plastic. Until you have removed a half-expelled but totally undigested Sainsbury's carrier bag from the arsehole of a highly distressed and very much astonished Great Dane you haven't lived.

The Houseworm clears up what's left, empties garbage, sorts and puts on laundry and turns to housework.

Start at the top, she said, and work down. So feather-dust ceilings and walls and pictures first, dust and polish surfaces second, and hoover the floors and carpets last.

Since even the most cursory performance of each of these tasks will take not less than an hour, you will appreciate the dangers of returning from the school run and rewarding yourself with a cup of coffee (by now cold) and a glance at the papers.

I not only do not have time for this, I do not have time, period. The daughter no longer gets collected from school at noon, thank God, so the Houseworm's commitment to dusting and polishing can continue uninterrupted until lunch, but there is a snag. While polishing the dining table, I find a silver-plate wine-coaster underneath it, still full of the third son's marbles. It needs cleaning, badly. So I take it to the cupboard where the silver polish ought to be but isn't, so that needs to go on the shopping list, and I notice that the hinge on the cupboard door is loose and so I go to the toolbox to get a screw driver, but remember I used it in the garden shed last week so I go and get it and it's lying next to the wheel-brace for the tractor which still needs its tyre changed so I decide I'll just finish that job while I'm here, and then, since the ground's still frozen, I reckon I can get a load of logs in so I start on that and by the time I break for lunch I have no idea who the bloody fool was who left all these clothes, feather dusters and tins of Old English Furniture Polish all over the dining-room table.

Since I didn't think to stop at twelve noon to stick potatoes in the oven, and since there's no time now to make soup, it looks like being bread, hummus (amazing recipe chapter 21!) and cheese again, which it is.

Unless the Househead, presently grinding out a thousand words a day from her arctic-simulator office over the garage, has a schedule that permits her to take HER dog for a walk, the thirty minutes after lunch are dedicated to the proposition that there is no activity on earth, even walking in the country on a lovely day, that cannot be utterly ruined by the presence of ten stone of moronic canine with a compulsion to demonstrate what an enthusiastic and affectionate character he has.

After pulling myself out of the all-but-frozen river and vainly attempting to disembowel the four-footed half-wit with a hawthorn branch, the rest of the day was to be available for further demonstrations of the superiority of the methodical male. Except that it is around now that the phone rings and a concerned teacher enquires as to who was supposed to collect the children this afternoon.

Arrival at the school, very late and extremely hacked off, should be an actor's dream come true, for the audience awaiting, with bated breath, my entrance on this occasion is three deep on the sidewalk and consists entirely of women. What a blaze of glory, eh? I mean they have stayed behind especially, this lot, so that a ragged and ironic cheer can greet me as I rush in to collect my daughter from a young female teacher whose half-smile and condescending eyes say it all.

What they say is, 'Isn't that typical of a man?' and they say it in any language without recourse to words, and the phenomenon is known as 'The Look' and you will be hearing a lot more about it. When I get back to the car the traffic warden has just finished. The traffic warden is not a bloke, and she can do 'The Look' as well, and she does. By now the daughter, who has long since perfected 'The Look', is saying, 'Are we going to be late for Joe?'

'What?'

'JOE . . . you know, JOE!'

I am not only half an hour late to collect him, but I have forgotten my third son's name.

He is sitting in a by now empty playground, totally engrossed in getting as much mud, grass and assorted crapola into his school uniform as the fibres of the material can retain. If I thought this was by way of punishment for my remiss behaviour I might think to apologize, but this is what he does every day. He then has to go and tell his teacher that his Dad 'FINALLY got here' and after being treated to this particular middle-aged woman's version of 'The Look', a bravura performance, incorporating the eyebrows of exasperation with the half-smile of pity and both covered with the profound knowledge that nothing will ever change, we can go home.

Halfway there the daughter's daily plea for a short pit-stop to take on a cold drink or an ice-cream or, if she can get it past me, one of each, has been reinforced in its powers of persuasion by parental guilt.

Also, since they both know the Househead by no means approves of treats of this nature, I'm hoping that they may forget to mention the fact that I was late. I drive home slowly so that by the time we turn up the evidence will have been consumed, and we pull up just as the Househead emerges from her office to find out what happened to her tea.

'MUMMYMUMMYGUESSWHATDADDYWAS-LATETOGETUSFROMSCHOOLANDWEHAD-ICECREAM*AND*COCA COLA!'

She looks at me. 'You forgot, didn't you.' This is not a question.

'Tea?' This *is* a question, but only just. More an 'Are we getting any . . .?' than a 'Would you like some. . . ?'

So now tea is served and the twin tasks of ensuring that Joe does his homework and Rosie is prevented from making more than four trips to the biscuit barrel before supper prove more than enough for the systematic, methodical and above all male approach to household management.

The parallel-thinking, multi-tasked female Chaos Theory apologists may very WELL have included at least some thought or even preparation for an evening meal between these two activities, but THEY wouldn't have been trying to read the paper which has sat, a silent rebuke, on the kitchen worktop all day. I mean, what's the point of buying it if you don't have time to read it? And do all washing-machines make that dreadful treble bleep over and over again until you empty them? Likewise tumble-dryers? AND THEY GO ON NO MATTER HOW LONG IT TAKES? Jesus, now I know why Isaac Asimov thought humans would be less than enthusiastic about being ruled by robots.

Rosie is now whinging that if she can't have a tenth and eleventh biscuit then natural justice dictates that she should be made 'pancakes with lemon AND sugar for her supper and not that bottled lemon juice either, and, Daddeee, how could you forget I told you BEFORE you went shopping that we needed lemons, why are you looking at me like that?'

So pancakes it is and while the batter sits in the fridge for a bit to contemplate its karma, now is the time to think about supper for bigger people. PANCAKES spring to mind. See, we have synergy!

The trouble, no, one of the many troubles with vegetarianism, apart from the fact that it's healthy, is what Paul Levy, of Oxford and the *Observer*, described as the Pale Brown Fart Food Factor. No matter how much the two-grand-a-day foodie photographer shifts the lights and adds the filters, the colour plates illustrating the most imaginative and delicious recipes for quiches, pulse pies, casseroles, nut loaves and bean burgers all come out looking like the food's bin ate once already. Exceptions to this rule are pastas and salads, but even then the most beautiful vegetarian tagliatelle or spinach and parmesan salad can still be improved by the addition of a few blush-pink prawns or crisp bits of bacon. What am I drooling on about? These things are in the past, and what I have to find now is something to put in the pancakes, which, when cooked, will resemble something to be eaten, rather than scraped off your shoe.

Another obstacle to be overcome by the harassed Houseworm is the fact that if I want some sort of black-eyed bean gloop to come pouring pungently out of each punctured pancake I SHOULD HAVE PUT THE BEANS ON TO SOAK JUST BEFORE BREAKFAST, and I didn't, did I?

Can't think why not . . . it's not as though the goings on around then were beyond the capacity of the organized, prioritized and sequential male-management structure.

So it's time to fall back on tinned tomatoes to make a thickish sauce in which I will envelop stir-fried bits of courgette, aubergine, celery, onion and, if I had any, courage, red, yellow and green peppers, but none of my vegetarian relations will eat them.

(A digression: does it not appear reasonable that all human beings are allowed their little quirks? Offal here, rice-pudding there, he won't eat liver, oysters make her queasy, you hate curry, I can live without chitterlings and my old man ate absolutely everything except Bombay Duck. But by the same token, once someone has foresworn ALL MEAT, ALL FISH, and sometimes eggs, cheese, butter and God knows what besides, THEIR OPTIONS HAVE ALL BEEN USED UP! There should not BE vegetarians who are picky about which vegetables they eat. They've used up their veto entitlement in one go and now they should eat what they're given, but no. No brassicas, no capsicums and nothing Chinese is the rule around here, and on every hand the Houseworm's scope for culinary imagination is being restricted.)

Back to pancakes. I'm trying to make the sauce thick enough to roll up in the pancakes and fry them crisp later while both children are eating pancakes slightly faster than I can cook them and a lot faster than I can sprinkle sugar and lemon juice on 'em. So Joe gets to do sugar (Rosie's idea of a fair helping being whatever amount we have in the house) and she does the lemon juice. This provides all sorts of opportunities for sibling score-settling and petty revenges which result in both children refusing to eat any pancake touched by the other and both bursting into tears of rage and frustration. It has, after all, been a long day. The upside of this is that they have, in fact, stopped eating their way through the pile of pancakes before the question of the thickness of the sauce became merely academic. At the same time we are trying to get the homework done, yes?

Leave sauce to cool, and chivvy two whacked and whinging combatants upstairs to the bath. The bath into which it is not FAIR that they should be forced and into which they are only indirectly coerced by the fact that Rosie sees in her brother's complaints the opportunity for earning Brownie points along the lines of 'Look at me. I'M getting in the bath, I'M being GOOD, aren't I, Joe's being BAD'. This, of course, results in Joe's rage increasing to shriek force 8 and my normal placid and patient disposition beginning to show signs of strain.

By the time they are both out, dried and in pyjamas, our version of the Victorian custom of the children being brought down for half an hour before bed is enacted. The Househead, if at home, gets called in from her office for a game of Happy Families or a chapter of Roald Dahl (EACH! One child is not prepared to be entertained by the other's story).

Teeth are cleaned, good nights said (several times), warnings against appearing downstairs issued, and it's hey for an evening of peace and quiet accompanied by the contents of the booze cupboard.

Not quite. The chickens have to be secured against the

depredations of the fox, the dog has to be taken out in a vain attempt to get him to perform somewhere further afield than the back porch, the third load of laundry (containing the set of school clothes the children will need tomorrow because I didn't include them all in last night's load) has to be set going, and by the time the Househead's drink has been poured and the sauce has cooled to the correct temperature, the dog has eaten the pancakes. This does not seem as funny to me as it might to the disinterested observer.

The only way out is to pretend that starting to peel potatoes for mash about twenty minutes before we intend to eat is what I had in mind all along; that's why I'm cutting them into tiny lumps so they'll cook faster, and that's why we're having frozen peas with the mash and the tomato gloop. Veg with veg is a way of life around here.

At least this plateful can be eaten with a fork in front of the nine o'clock news, which has to be watched every night just in case the Thatcher–Lamont–Baker axis has finally turned the Househead's Prime Ministerial biography into a posthumous analysis of The Fall of Major.

The joy of a fork-only supper is that you can eat without having to put your glass down between mouthfuls. This accelerates the slide into oblivion that you have been looking forward to since 6.30 a.m., and oblivion happily intrudes even before John Kettley has started gibbering on about low-pressure areas. However, the coma induced is insufficiently deep to obscure the distant 'beep beep beep' of a washing-machine proudly telling me how clever it's been. Stagger through to kitchen, clear up mess in a haze of indignation, put washing in tumble-dryer, forget to switch the thing on and go to bed. Meet wife on the way.

'Are you OK?' Tender concern all over. 'Time to send for Superman?'

'No,' I slur. 'This isn't a job for Superman . . . This,' I say, 'is a job for a WOMAN!'

I don't remember anything else.

CHAPTER FIVE

Action and Reaction

'There's obviously something wrong with him ...
perhaps the size?'

CARMEN CALLIL

IN FEBRUARY I WAS A GUEST AT A DINNER IN SCOTLAND,
hosted by one of the most successful businessmen in the
country. Also present were the MD of Hilton Hotels in the
Far East, his wife, who ran her own business doing trade
with mainland China, the founder of a Madison Avenue
advertising agency, and my sister, 1991's Businesswoman
of the Year (who had kindly wheeled me in among the
great and the good; otherwise this was no place for a
Houseworm).

By way of chat, she mentioned that as well as having an

interest in a catering business, I was actually occupied full time in looking after four children and a house and garden while my wife brought home the bacon.

Silence.

'No, really. He cooks, cleans, does the laundry, the school run, everything.'

Silence.

Fortunately she was distracted before she felt compelled to get a response by telling the assembled throng how I cleaned 'RIGHT ROUND THE BEND!'

These people had absolutely no way of reacting to this information. She might as well have told them I suffered from an unfortunate bowel condition. Not even a chilly 'How interesting' could cope with a breach of etiquette of this magnitude, but all of them had children, kitchen tables and dirty socks to deal with.

To discuss a fairly novel, though increasingly common, method of dealing with them was a gaffe. Interestingly, in this bastion of chauvinism, the businessman had just appointed his daughter to the job of running the family firm, and her three brothers report to her. (She, of course, still reports to HIM!) I asked her later who did her housework, and she told me not to be silly, who but she COULD do it?

I sometimes pause, arms immersed in washing-up, to consider the truly great questions about life, the universe, and how did I get into this and who cares and why me?

Then I pull myself together and take her up a cup of coffee. She's only been working for four hours, during which time I have cleaned the WHOLE kitchen. Sort of.

'Seen this?'

She's got one of her silent chortle faces on.

She shows me.

A recent poll by some employment consultancy showed that out of 226 women from over fifty different firms, nearly 80 per cent thought that any man in a traditionally female job (secretary? nurse?) had something wrong with their sexuality.

'OK, Winifred?' she says. 'If you think you're slowing down at all, have you considered HRT?'

I don't dignify this sort of macho posturing with a reply. It wasn't ME who was standing outside the airing cupboard at 2 a.m. after flying in from two eighteen-hour days in Manchester, refolding the children's underpants.

'It's just that, um, they don't LOOK right the way you fold them,' she'd said. FOLD them? We are talking underpants here. Does having something wrong with my sexuality lead to inadequate Y-front configuration? Or is it that my sexuality is insufficiently warped to make me know the RIGHT way to fold underpants? Finally, she said she didn't know what had come over her, and she wouldn't do it again. When I found her putting extra blankets on the children, and swapping the cuddly toys I'd left with them for different ones, she claimed she'd been sleepwalking.

My mother, a classic example of the success of talent regardless of sex, has been heard to mutter, after a glass or two, that a man changing nappies 'ain't fittin'!' She says it in her Annie Oakley voice to take the sting out of it, but she definitely has a few niggling little reservations.

This, I am convinced, comes from her devotion to my father, now alas dead, whose idea of a good time was winding up the Neanderthals who were forever asking him how he could possibly 'allow his wife to work'. He used to say that as soon as she was earning enough he was going to become a kept man and devote his remaining years to eating his way round Europe at her expense. In South Africa, in the 1950s, this sort of sedition could induce apoplexy.

BUT, in twenty-five years of marriage, he had never had cause to know where the teacups, let alone the tea, were kept, and he made damn sure he never found out. As for changing a nappy, he often remarked that children were simply an assimilation of uncontrolled orifices, but the idea that he might deal with the requirements of any of them never, ever, crossed his mind.

When it finally crossed mine, I went happily about expecting praise and tribute from every female within bouquet-throwing range. Finally, I thought, I've cracked it. Tom Cruise eat your heart out: I am every woman's dream come true. Hah.

There is something deep in the heart, or soul, or womb of even the most committed career feminist that knows that having a man muscling in on hearth and home and children is deeply, disturbingly and disastrously WEIRD.

You may think you're dusting the pictures, but she knows that she is scraping panther droppings off the wall of her personal primeval cave, and that if she doesn't do it right the panther will come back and devour her children.

Before I became a full-time Houseworm and learned to love the laundry, I was occasionally to be found on secondment to the childcare division during the Househead's temporary absences among the megabucks.

On one such occasion it was 'playgroup day'.

'You don't have to take him,' she'd said, 'I'll arrange to take him on Thursday instead.'

She has always known precisely how to wind me up. I was immediately determined to take him, just as she would have done had she been here, and since she would have done it without my help, I determined to manage this simple task alone, and without mentioning it further.

On reflection, it might have been a good idea to ask where the playgroup was held, but having merely grunted, I was later reduced to ringing another mother to find out.

Caroline is a local councillor, a lecturer in politics, and married to an accountant. When I called, instead of telling me where the playgroup met, she asked if Penny was ill or something.

'No, just breadwinning.'

'Oh,' she sounded doubtful. Then, 'Tell you what . . . I'll come and pick him up on my way!'

Helpful though this sounds, I had my reservations about Joe's enthusiasm for being picked up and driven off to playgroup by a woman he'd maybe seen twice in his life before, if that.

I protested that I was rather hoping to walk up to the village with Joe in the buggy, and if she would just tell me where to go, we'd see her there.

'Nonsense, I'll come and get him!'

Through clenched teeth I declared my enthusiasm for a walk and demanded directions, and in a by now pretty huffy voice, induced no doubt by my ingratitude, she told me.

Her umbrage didn't last long, however. Joe and I arrived expecting that I would spend an hour amongst other parents while he spent an hour doing developmentally correct, socially interactive things like pushing, shoving, crying and getting the crap beaten out of him by a three-year-old female thug half his size.

Caroline was waiting at the door of the church hall. To the innocent observer she would have appeared to be guarding it.

'OK,' she said, as I got Joe out of the buggy, 'I'll take him in and you can come back and get him in an hour!', and she started to peel him off me.

At this, needless to say, Joe wrapped both arms and both legs round me and screamed blue murder. This was not a great introduction to playgroup for either of us. Eventually, I was allowed to take him in, but only with Caroline operating on the assumption that as soon as he was 'settled', I'd sneak off.

'After all, you must have lots of better things to do.'

This is a recurring theme of housewormery. I didn't; and I didn't sneak off, either, but I didn't go to playgroup again.

For 'other parents' read 'mothers', with the occasional nanny or au pair thrown in, and my arrival caused something of a hiatus in the middle of the Gold Blend and gynaecology.

One hour of whispers and giggles ensued at the periphery

of my perception, while in the foreground Caroline made small talk with a frozen smile on her face that told me she was going to be blamed for letting me in. I couldn't inflict that on her again, and, come to think of it, I was damned if I was going to inflict it on myself.

I'm sure that 'infant socialization' is an educational necessity among the politically correct, but the sisters draw the line at fathers' involvement. Under these circumstances a thirty-year-old woman barrister with three children under ten will feel more at ease with a seventeen-year-old Turkish au pair girl with no English, no children and no brains than she would with another barrister with children of identical ages if the second legal eagle was a bloke.

Gynaecology has a lot to answer for.

Some years later I discovered that nothing had changed.

Where Joe and Rosie go to school there is a morning ritual enacted that is as old as time itself; for generations mothers have met and chatted, and the only difference is that the well or the wash-house has been replaced by the school dropping-off point and the open door of the Volvo.

The fact that the ritual ensures that the carefully designed one-way system, meant to ensure the smooth arrival, set down and (immediate) departure of each delivering parent, backs up across half of Surrey has no more effect on Joan's and Catherine's discussion of who should visit whom later that same morning for coffee than the fact that they both have telephones. Delivering fathers, late for trains, appointments or assessment interviews with the Chairman, may swear, raise eyes ostentatiously to heaven or even hoot, but they are invisible and inaudible and irrelevant. This is female territory, and inviolable.

They're not just fixing up their coffee mornings, either. There are child-minding arrangements for pre-school children so that mothers can have days away on courses, lovers or shopping expeditions. School runs are organized, tennis games arranged and, above all, there are the discussion groups on obstetrics and gynaecology. I don't feel badly about being excluded from these last, but other than that, I have everything in common with these people, but the exclusion is total.

I had been delivering Joe just about every day for six months when I was approached by a mum.

'Does your wife ever deliver in the mornings?'

'Not unless I can't; can I help?'

'No, it's OK. I just wanted to see if she'd be interested in sharing a school run . . . I'll ring her at home.'

I am not making this up.

Teachers, too, are locked into this charade.

'Now, Rosie, don't forget to tell your mummy you need a name tape on your tunic,' is addressed to her in my presence as though I'm not there, even though they may not yet have MET Rosie's mother and the child has been brought to school and collected by me every morning and afternoon. I suspect they think that if they ask me to see a name tape gets sewn on, I'll go home and shout at the wife.

It was a year of delivering and collecting at the school gates before more than half the mothers would return my cheery morning greeting. I stuck at this with a grim determination. I wanted to see how long they could hold out. Eventually we reached the stage where those mothers whose children had been over to our house to play would be prepared to talk to me outside the gates for all the world as though I was human. Or female?

I taxed one of them with all this female chauvinism.

'Well, you must admit, it's pretty odd. Haven't you got anything better to do?'

'Haven't you?'

'Of course not. I have to look after the children.' Such self-esteem, yet.

The ice being broken, I dared to ask why I was regarded with such suspicion.

'Oh, don't be so silly.'

'No, really. What does a bloke have to do?'

She was, I swear, on the point of saying, 'Get a job, I suppose,' when she realized what job she'd got.

'You can be the home-person,' she finally said, 'but the group at the school gate is exclusive not to housepeople, but to women . . . and I don't think you want to be one of those, or do you?'

Gobsmacked I was, but she was right.

Life ain't easy for a boy named Sue.

There's a solution to this non-acceptance ritual, but in my case it's a price too high to pay. You want the ice-bitch from hell to smile at you as if she remembers that she's seen you every day for a year? Take the dog to school with you.

It will come as no surprise that the same people who treat the 'umble 'ouseworm with all the contempt and contumely he deserves for being the pathetic, intrusive excuse for a man that he is, will immediately start simpering and slobbering over a flatulent Great Dane who REALLY hasn't got any balls and whom they've never seen in their lives before. 'Ooooh, isn't he lovely,' you hear them cry. 'What's his name? Have you had him long? How old is he? Blahblahblah' . . . all this from those wonderful people who brought you the 'Drop dead, creep' stare and the 'Who's this invisible guy to tell me good-morning' response. It's the attraction of opposites . . . they're all horrible in different ways.

Still, there was always a warm kernel of comfort to be derived from the knowledge that I was at the cutting edge of enlightenment, and that new men, like prophets, may well be without honour in their own land.

It wasn't until I met Sarah that I realized that what I was doing was 'functionalizing my envy and resentment of women by superficially going along with what I imagined was the feminist ideal whereas my very nature meant that I had no ability to comprehend feminism and whether I knew it or not my domestic arrangements were a usurpation of my wife's rights and responsibilities.'

At least, I think that was what she said, but I sort of lost track after 'functionalizing'.

What I said was, 'Huh?'

Sarah is quiet, intense and deeply committed. *Should* be committed is the way I see it.

Her husband, which may explain a lot, will, by the year 2000, be the last unreconstituted Male Chauvinist Pig out of captivity.

'You're a smug bugger,' she said, when I was admittedly preening myself over my sexual enlightenment and domestic self-confidence.

'Do you know ANYTHING about feminism?' she says.

'Not a lot, but I make a really great soufflé, and there's not a lot you can tell me about nappy rash.'

She didn't seem to see the relevance, somehow.

CHAPTER SIX

Totentanz

'The car, the furniture, the wife, the children – everything has to be disposable. Because you see, the main thing today is – shopping.'

ARTHUR MILLER

BY A THIRD OF THE WAY THROUGH THE MAJOR YEAR, I'D got shopping sussed.

Mr Neanderthal used to go to work in the forest every day while Mrs N. and the kids stayed home for the very good reason that he was stronger, faster and, above all, a lot dumber than she was; and if anybody was going to dispute possession of the corpse of a rock hyrax with a sabre-toothed tiger, she had long since identified the boy for the job.

By alternately telling him what a mighty hunter he was, how she made the best rock hyrax stew in the business, and how rock hyrax stew made her 'really HOT, y'know . . .', she ensured that Mr N. was out there in all weathers giving the sabre-tooth a good deal of uphill.

As soon as rock hyrax stew became just another item on the Sainsbury's low-cal microwavable meals list for October, Mrs N. persuaded the old man that his aggression, strength and speed would be better applied in obtaining reverse take-over equity finance from Sabre-tooth PLC and leave the shopping to her.

Those women who missed each other in the school car-park have another territory sacred to the pursuit of female social intercourse, and it's called Tesco or Waitrose or Safeway and it's THEIRS. It remains theirs right up until 5 p.m., after which men are admitted without question because they have clearly received instructions to pick up the steaks on the way home. Men are NOT regarded with equanimity at 10.45 a.m. when they are 'excuse me-ing' their way down aisles filled to capacity with the stationary trolleys of long-lost friends (long-lost ever since nine fifteen that morning) discussing the shortcomings of their husbands, HRT or the F-Plan diet, or all three.

We have a fool-proof (this means me, apparently) shopping method at our house. Whenever somebody opens the last packet, tin or whatever of anything, they write it down on the always available list by the telephone in the kitchen.

Once a week, someone phones up for someone who's out, and whoever takes the message writes it on the only available piece of blank paper in the joint, namely the reverse of the shopping list. The person to whom the message is addressed then picks up this piece of paper, takes it off somewhere either to respond from a more private extension or to write down the number elsewhere, and then throws it away. This means that prior to every shopping expedition it is necessary to visit every stockpile from the lavatory paper and tissues in the upstairs landing cupboard to the bags of mixed corn in the chicken shed, by way of the non-biological washing liquid in the utility room and the cockatiel mix in the play-room fireplace, pen and paper in hand. This all takes a great deal of time and, like the brush-salesman's patter, if I get interrupted I have to start again from the top because I can never remember if it's not on the list because we've got some or because I've forgotten to check.

Eventually I have a list that resembles nothing more than a stores requisition form for a three-week cruise on the *QE2*. Then I shout up the stairs to the Householder for her addenda. These invariably include either Lil-lets, panty-shields or both. 'Sure you've got the right size, sir? hee! hee!'

(Note: Do not, under any circumstances, respond to this merry jape with, 'Actually I'm not sure . . . my wife's about your size, can you try one for me?' You can get arrested for less.)

Checking the whole thing one last time because this is going to be the week when NOTHING gets forgotten and I won't have to schlepp back into town on Saturday morning, I collect the ecologically sound trolley-bags from the pantry, make sure I've got money AND plastic, pick up the car keys and set off, making absolutely sure that in doing so I leave the shopping list on the kitchen table.

The worst thing about this is not that I will miss out some of the items on the list (I do that even if I've got the blasted thing with me) but that when I get back she will be standing in the kitchen with the list in her hand and a smirk on her face saying that if you're going to forget something she guesses the shopping list sort of covers all the options. I could always go back for it, but she'll bring it out to me, smiling sweetly the while; so that rules that out.

Mr Memory, that's me. At least from a start like this my performance, like that of the England cricket squad or the Tory government, can only get better. Waitrose, here I come.

There is a definite, observable difference between the shopping methods of men and women. The latter write lists of exclusively staple, sensible and necessary items, buy everything on the list and then buy one of everything else in the shop 'just in case'. Men write lists, leave them at home, buy half the items that were on the list (NOT the sensible, essential half), and then cruise the aisles for luxuries like smoked oysters, English asparagus and proper sausages (you remember . . . the ones with meat in them). And what they buy is dictated entirely by how hungry they are when forced to do the shopping. Furthermore, the returning female of the species wants no more from her spouse than help getting all her acquisitions out of the car and into the kitchen. What the returning male requires is praise, delighted astonishment and even applause. I cannot understand why my own dear helpmeet has been heard to remark that if there's one thing that gets up her pipe, it's being required to clap as I produce the extra virgin olive oil with the self-satisfied air of a conjuror with a white rabbit.

I'm told this is usual. It goes back to Mr N. and his rock hyrax. After all, who's got the most interesting tale to tell? He with his sabre-tooth derring do, or she with six hours spent pounding maize and sweeping the cave?

Prior to my departure, and, I would argue, the cause of my momentary lapse in the matter of the shopping list, I have collected into the back of the car all our carefully collected recyclables which in our house means newspapers and bottles. Especially bottles. Bottles in quantities sufficient to mean that our decision to recycle is based less on political correctness than on a profound desire to avoid the censure of the dustmen, sorry . . . waste disposal operatives. The sound of clanking empties rising through the bathroom window first thing in the morning is frequently accompanied by gasps of disbelief and shouts of, 'Bloody hell . . . look at this: two cases of plonk since last time. Don't you reckon someone should tell 'em if they drank less they could afford some quite nice claret!'

So it's off to the bottle/paper bank first, simply in order to make room in the car for the shopping. Why is it that local councils were so keen to be seen to be green (for a small fee

that assonant bit of creative genius may be available to the
brothers Saatchi) that they omitted to allow funds for the
emptying of bottle banks at sufficiently short intervals? This
oversight allows the bins to overflow, dissatisfied punters
then leave cardboard boxes full of empties around the base
of each bin, and at one o'clock in the morning the local
youf can amuse themselves by hurling this stockpile of free
ammunition into the road and laying bets on which sort of
bottle explodes most spectacularly. Either on the Tarmac or
upside some other yobbo's head.

I calculate that since the introduction of ecologically
desirable bottle banks, the amount of carbon dioxide, heavy
metals and general pollution released into the atmosphere by
the cars of those making special trips to offload their empties
only to find they can't, and the nuisance and aural pollution
caused by hurling green bottles into the green bin, brown
into the brown, white into the white and any left over into
the garden opposite has guaranteed that the ecology will
hold up, just, until next Thursday.

In the mean time, I am trying to find somewhere
to park.

There is always the back of the supermarket car-park,
but to go straight there, and have to queue, probably, is
an admission of defeat. What I want is a place bang outside
the front doors of Waitrose, and there's a reason for this.

Once, long ago, when times were a lot better than they
are now, the woman I married got it into her head that our
whole family should be treated to an outing to London and
a visit to Harrods. This was on the last Saturday morning
before Christmas, exactly one year before the IRA had the
same idea.

'Are you crazy?', 'We won't be able to park closer than
Hammersmith' and 'the place will be heaving' and 'let's not'
all fell on deaf ears.

'Just watch,' she said. 'Relax,' she said. 'Leave it to me.'

At precisely 10.30 a.m. she pulled into the only empty
parking space in London west of Traitor's Gate, on the

corner of Knightsbridge and Hans Crescent, 17 feet (I measured it) from Harrods' side entrance. I have not been allowed to forget this, and I am convinced that God is storing up some real humdinger of a disaster for her and her last words will be something about there being a price to pay for all the parking spaces.

She can't miss, and it's got to the stage now that I tell anyone who will listen that if they have difficulty parking they should tell the Almighty that they're a friend of Penelope's, and lo and behold . . .

These people are now coming back to me without the cynical sneer and asking if Penelope minds being a friend of some friends of theirs as well.

In the end, of course, I have to go round to the back of Waitrose and queue up fifty cars back from where I would have been if I had put less trust in the Almighty's pro-Penny position and gone there at the start. I'm beginning to suspect that the quid pro quo for all HER parking places will not be some mega-disaster to come, but the constant denial of her husband so much as a meter with some unexpired time on it.

Into battle: I have obtained one trolley and in it, so far, are two empty trolley-bags, and I am now going to re-demonstrate the male system . . . start in one corner of the supermarket and work your way stolidly around the store covering every aisle until you end up back where you started (*see below:* Tom Peters and Serial Management). By this means you will have seen every product in the shop and been reminded of the contents of the list that is even now causing your wife to splutter merrily into her morning coffee. There are two drawbacks to this system: 1) You end up with a trolley that has eggs, yoghurt cartons and butter at the bottom with tinned tomatoes and cases of wine and mineral water on top. By the time you reach the checkout what you've got is a trail of scrambled egg and yoghurt behind you and two pound of butter soaking into the wire mesh of trolley.

2) Your eye will be caught by something two aisles across that you know was on the list and once you've broken the system to get it, you've forgotten where you were. This is because the background music, colour scheme and product layout of all supermarkets, together with the uniforms and tones of voice of the staff, are designed to induce in shoppers the sort of brain-dead catatonia that allows them to load up their trolleys without making a single connection between action and cost. That's why they take switch cards.

So what you do is head for where you know the regular items, the staples you buy every week, have been stacked for as long as you can remember. I mean THIS you can do on automatic pilot, right? Wrong!

Lest any of the undead shoppers have somehow managed to retain one operative brain cell, the supermarket manager has arranged for every single item in the store to be shuffled round, so that all those mean sunsabitches who simply buy what they need now have to schlepp round the whole store before they can locate the sliced white. In the process, four out of five dumb Houseworms will see something they have absolutely no need for, no enthusiasm about and no intention of buying, and buy it.

'I thought it might be nice to try tinned Guatemalan spider fruit' is not going to get you excused 'The Look'.

With me it's the grog. It's got so the wine department in this little local supermarket have started sending me invitations to tastings. They certainly know when they're onto a good thing . . . you can see them nodding and smiling at each other as my trolley rounds cakemaker's corner heading for the Wine of the Month.

''Ere, Simon, don't rush off. This gennleman'll want a couple cases up from the warehouse, won't you, sir?' That stops most of the supermarket's braindead in their tracks.

'Oooo, having a party, are we?'

It's easier to say 'yes' than face the censure by confessing that this is a week's consumption where I come from.

Half the local population are convinced we give wild

parties every week and the friends through to whom this intelligence has filtered are friends no longer because they know they haven't been invited once in six months.

Supermarket trolleys have been ergonomically (whatever that is) designed. This, apparently, ensures that they are just sufficiently large to be impossible to manoeuvre when fully laden, while remaining just small enough to ensure that the top three items, which you have taken great pains to ensure are things that would break if anything is piled on top of them, fall off and break.

There is no way round this. If you put heavy things at the bottom, they're last out at the checkout and therefore last into the trolley as you head for the car-park. And vice versa.

If I have given insufficient incentive for my fellow man to eschew all forms of housewormery but especially shopping, try to imagine facing the supermarket during the school holidays, when YOU HAVE TO TAKE YOUR CHILDREN WITH YOU!

Now we have all seen, have we not, the harassed young mother of three children below the age of five attempting to get the weekly shopping done in spite of their attempts to steer the trolley into her legs, tip the baby out of it and steal the sweets that the thoughtful supermarket manager has placed so conveniently to hand for them. The crafty sod ought to be done for aiding and abetting. Her method of dealing with these trying circumstances is usually to yell at them first, and, having detected no improvement within a millisecond or so, to lay about her and into them with an enthusiasm that would gladden the heart of W.C. Fields. Her children are now screaming the place down, and the more they yell the more she clunks them and so on, and all around her other mothers are clucking in sympathy because they know how tough it is, and female eyeballs are rolling heavenwards in a heartwarming display of sisterly solidarity.

Now; I took my then four-year-old daughter shopping

one day (not a mega-shop, you understand, just a few things) and while waiting for the checkout body to ring them up, she was standing on the end of the counter (my daughter, not the checkout person) and falling off so that I could catch her.

She likes this game.

Not so the army of female shoppers, all of whom could spot the symptoms of incipient child abuse a mile off. You could have heard the 'Tsks! Tsks!' all down the high street, and mutterings along the lines of 'Typical man!' and 'Honestly, some people!' and 'You'd think he'd be more responsible!' were reaching a level at which I deemed it best to leave before the social workers' sirens awoke the whole town to my wickedness.

Once the switch card has been applied, the happy Houseworm has only to negotiate the car-park without allowing his trolley to capsize over the carefully positioned drain covers, gullies and Tarmac ramps a thoughtful supermarket chain has designed into the layout, load up the car and go home in the by now pouring rain.

EXCEPT there is still the bread shop, the butcher, the dry-cleaner, the hardware shop and the delicatessen that sells some things the supermarket has decided the great unwashed aren't quite ready for: pecorino cheese, for example, or those deep-fried, salsa-flavoured crisps (so delicious you can feel them doing you harm) or Californian olives stuffed with whole garlic cloves. Yes, I know, but if you have a jar of them all to yourself who needs friends?

So I stack up the car and set off on the other errands, remembering at all times that the time taken is being measured all over the car's upholstery by the melting coefficient of butter.

And another thing: how come I absolutely cannot bring myself to buy convenience grub? I go out to dinner with friends and marvel at the elegance of the tagliatelle with mushrooms, the salmon en croute and the mixed leaves salad with orange and chicory, and the host/hostess says,

'I picked it all up at Marks and Spencer an hour ago.' Has this person no shame? Apparently not, and as far as I can see they've got their heads screwed on a great deal straighter than I have, but I can't do it.

Work, and most especially cooking, will inevitably expand to fill the available time and space. Any sensible Houseworm with some work study awareness and delusions of adequacy in the time management department would price their time, deduct the cost of the extra two hours of cooking boeuf bourguignon from scratch from the price of the deep-frozen, ready-to-eat, serves-six little number in the supermarket freezer, deduct the cost of the raw materials, allowing double quantities because sure as hell if you don't burn the first attempt the dog will get it, and you'll find that by going for a convenience pack you are saving yourself about fifty quid a day, and at that rate who cares what the muck tastes like. BUT I CAN'T DO IT.

I suspect that there's something primeval about it, so that sissies who cook, like me (and Keith Floyd, Michel Roux, Nico Ladenis and Marco Pierre White, of course), don't feel right unless we're directly responsible for the expressions of bliss on the faces of their customers and revulsion on the faces of my children.

So the trolley that I have wrestled through the pouring rain contains not only enough food for a week but enough work for a fortnight.

Shopping is a pain, and, like all pains, is best gotten over with in one intense burst rather than by absorbing a little errand each day like some sort of Chinese water torture. I will, however, be back. While I was concentrating on the relative scores of aubergines as against courgettes in the YUK-factor gastronomy of my children, I forgot the Lil-lets.

CHAPTER SEVEN

Real Men

'Women are really much nicer than men: no wonder we like them.'

KINGSLEY AMIS

PICTURE THIS, IF YOU WILL. I AM STANDING IN OUR kitchen, where I have spent most of the day, what with one thing and another, and I am preparing a small plate of spaghetti with melted cheese on top for an invalid. The invalid in question is my grandchild, born five minutes earlier to my five-year-old daughter, and represented by a singularly unappealing cabbage-patch doll. Do all five-year-old girls do this? Rosie is capable of 'giving birth' to three doll daughters (never sons), two small furry animals and a hot-water bottle in as many minutes. She then requires that I should look after them as I would my own, and no matter how deeply committed I may be to this game, she can change the rules faster than I can keep up.

'No, Daddeee, THAT's Emily! LORNA's the one with the sore leg! You need to get a bandage, an' Sophie's got to have some 'getti, 'cos she's got flu. She likes it with cheese, not tomato sauce.'

While I am extracting blazing spaghetti and melted cheese from the microwave, and burning my thumb in the process ('Daddeee, don't say naughty words in front of the children'), I am entering into the spirit of the thing and saying, 'I'm sorry you're not well, Sophie. Do you think you'd like a little warm milk to help you get your strength back?'

At this moment the door opens and Macho Michael, the housewives' heartthrob and all-round jack-the-lad, sticks his head in to see if I can play tennis on Friday. Did he hear? I bluff it out and hand him the doll. 'Hold Sophie for a minute, will you, Mike? She's not well. I'll get you a beer.' He jumps back as though I've handed him a rattlesnake.

'Not likely, Marigold. I'm not going to turn out a woofter like you!'

He never learns. Years ago, when our number-one son was about fifteen, Mike came in to find Joe, the number-three item, involved in a complicated fantasy based on two Ninja turtles and two of his sister's dolls. 'What on earth are you doing, Joe? Only girls play with dolls. You don't want to turn out like your dad, you know! What are you playing with dolls for?'

Number One looked up from his book. 'I think he's practising to be a father. What are you practising for with all those men at the rugby club?' I promptly confirmed all Mike's suspicions by whooping with delight and hugging my eldest son till he said, 'Ow gerroff. Mike thinks you're funny enough as it is.' I suspect that Mike delivered *his* son to his boarding prep school aged seven, shook him manfully by the hand and hasn't hugged him since. Oh well.

'What are you doing here? I thought you were away on a course this week.' Mike is one of life's competitors. Management Development Courses, Sales Conferences, Leadership Weekends in the Brecon Beacons are all grist to his mill.

'Got back early,' he leers. 'Wife thinks I'm away till tomorrow, fnarr, fnarr! Bet you wish you could get a pink ticket for one of our management courses . . . think how efficiently you'd get the laundry done!'

Surprisingly, I have an answer for this, but it's probably not worth taking him on. I pour him a beer and listen to the details of the latest business management theories, and the latest analyses of the multi-billion-dollar success story that makes up CNN, Microsoft and Ross Perot's Electronic Data Systems.

'The thing is,' he says, 'the rate of change out there is so fast now that to keep one jump ahead you have to make decisions about six different things at once. It's no good dealing with things one step at a time . . . you have to keep on top of a lot of different areas simultaneously!'

'You mean like a housewife?' Mike doesn't bother to notice this.

'We had two seminars last week that demonstrated how we have to make decisions based on verbal communications and immediate action. Like when you're out on the edge and your team depends on you and you've got no time to call a meeting. That's why these courses are so important.'

'You mean like when Rosie's got a temperature of 102, the car's broken down, Penny's in Manchester and the cat's just dumped in the laundry basket? I shouldn't bother to call a meeting? I should just establish priorities, make a decision and get onto the next thing?'

'Yah that's it, you just . . . what are you on about? I'm talking about WORK, here.'

It seems a pity to tease him really, but the poor sap could have got all this from doing a bit of houseworming, and saved himself the expense of seminars, self-help text-books and survival weekends in February. The joke is, of course, that management psychologists have identified that what industry really needs are parallel-thinking, multi-tasked, instant-decision-making managers for what the guru of them all, Tom Peters, calls the nano-second nineties. Namely, mothers. Or Houseworms, even. But not me. I'm too busy with domestic trivia to spend any time putting IBM back on the rails.

Saturday morning in suburbia should be the management paradigm.

Consider: by tacit agreement, she will do the shopping while he mows the lawn.

What she is actually doing is this: clearing up breakfast, changing the baby's nappy, making the beds, putting on the laundry, driving the older child to her swimming lesson, doing the shopping, driving home, putting the shopping away, making him a cup of coffee, preparing the lunch, fetching the budding swimmer, hanging out the washing, pouring the old man a 'well-deserved' beer and serving the lunch.

What *he*'s actually doing is this: mowing the lawn.

Now I've been enjoying the role generally played by the character in the skirt in the above vignette. The only difference being that when I've finished MY Saturday morning, I get to spend the afternoon mowing the lawn.

The Houseworm's business technique has only one management law, which is 'the day will not be without surprises', and only one objective: to get through it.

The Editorial Director of Cable Network News operates by this principle as well, and in 1991 the company made $167 million.

Mike, by this time, has thought of something.

'Did you see that you're only worth £18,000 to the wife? Legal and General did a breakdown.'

According to these daft 'erberts that's what you get if you add up the hours spent doing the ironing, say, or the childcare, and apply the commercial rate for the job. No-one at Legal and General appears to have thought that maybe some of these tasks are carried out simultaneously.

They obviously don't have a Houseworm on the Board. (No, nor a woman neither.)

What they do have is the outdated idea that the way to get things done is to concentrate on the task in hand and when you've finished that, go on to the next one. So THAT'S how you can get to stay at work twelve hours a day, six days a week and call in on Sundays!

Soon there won't be 18 pence, let alone £18,000, for that sort of time-wasting nonsense.

Most men are saps. They set out to earn the living that will allow them to marry, breed and continue to eat; and they end up complaining that work has to take precedence, that their wives don't understand them, that they don't understand their children and if they have any spare time they'd rather spend it with other men, frequently those with whom they've just been working, and about whom, when they get home to the wife, they will spend most time complaining.

After they've woken her up, that is.

By this time I have bandaged, dosed and fed not only Rosie's children, but her and her brother as well, and Mike is rapidly moving on to his third beer. I ask after his wife.

'Fine,' he says. 'Only she's not talking to me again. So not all bad, eh? D'you understand women? I don't understand bloody women.'

I say, 'What's so difficult to understand?' and he says, 'You *would* say that . . . you *are* a bloody woman.'

So I trail the troops up the stairs to the bath with Mike muttering along behind. 'You know what my wife wants? Says she wants a job. A job, fer chrissake. Who's going to look after the house? What's she need a job for? Great house, three kids away at school, nothing to do all day. Says she's got no status; says people are only defined by their work and why don't housewives get salaries. Penny pays you, does she?'

I tell him no. I tell him we've got a partnership deal, and like most partnerships we have a partnership account and either of us can sign the cheques.

'You've got a joint account? Why? You don't earn any money.'

I tell him that I do what I do so Penny CAN earn money, and that's why we share the proceeds.

'Penny must be crazy,' he says.

By this time he's watching me transfer the contents of the laundry basket to the airing cupboard while I simultaneously yell at the children to get off the loo, get undressed and get into the bath.

'Can't remember ever bathing my kids,' he says. 'Do you actually enjoy it . . . all this domestic rubbish?'

I may be imagining it, but to me Macho Mike is beginning to sound the tiniest bit wistful.

'Folding socks? You must be kidding. But it does have its consolations. Like I get to decide what's for supper (Oh, God, that reminds me!), and the children are fun, and I don't have to answer to some whizkid boss who thinks anyone leaving the office before 9 p.m. isn't fully committed. Also, Penny works from home a lot, so we see more of each other than most couples, but that might not suit you, of course.'

He says he'd love to see more of Penny, hur, hur, and then he goes downstairs and gets us another beer, while I insist that washing, too, can be a part of bath-time. I also hang up towels that tradition dictates are left soaking wet on the floor of the bathroom after use, and attempt to convince two smalls that eleven seconds holding a toothbrush and showing off for Mike's benefit will not earn either of them the dental hygienist's 'I'm a Plaque Attaquer' badge on their next visit.

'Can Mike play "Hearts"?' Joe wants to know.

Mike says he has to meet someone, then Rosie says

'pleeease' and Mike forgets about someone and succumbs. We play cards sitting on our bed, and in the middle of it Penny comes home and joins in and then after the children are left upstairs to decide for themselves, as usual, when they'll go to bed and start sleeping, Mike is still hanging about looking bemused.

Penny, by this time, is mouthing 'What's he doing here?' faces at me and shaking her head vigorously when I make 'More beer?' faces back. It was probably a mistake on Mike's part to line up his empties on the worktop quite so conspicuously.

Suddenly he says, 'Is that Rosie?' and dives back up the stairs making giant growly noises, and can be heard pursuing our daughter back to her bed amid shrieks of delight and cries of 'No! No!' meaning 'Yes! Yes!' that are likely to get her thrown out of the Women's Movement when she's older.

Mike reappears. 'Any more beer? Or do I have to go?' Not even the Executive Woman can resist this 'little boy lost' performance and he gets invited to supper. 'There's enough, isn't there?' she says. 'Enough of what?' say I, and we spend some quality time debating the dietary needs of vegetarian telly presenters as opposed to the constant availability of pasta.

'Pasta?' says Mike. 'I do the best pasta in the world. Step aside, Marigold, and I'll show you some real cooking! Got any garlic?'

THIS, the wife and I both decide telepathically, we have GOT to see, and sit and watch while he goes into his act. It's an act because ever since he saw Michael Caine in *The Ipcress File*, he's got it into his head that one of the most sure-fire ways to make a woman go all weak at the knees is to invite her over, and then instead of jumping on her before she's got her coat off, cooking her exotic and fascinating food and demonstrating what a fully rounded Renaissance man you are. Pasta is as exotic as Mike gets. Once he got MARRIED, of course, he needed a road map to find the kitchen.

MACHO MIKE'S KNOCK 'EM DEAD PASTA
(Serves two)

Take 200 gms of pasta, boil in salted water until *al dente*. Meanwhile, take one head (yup, really: about twelve cloves) of garlic, and chop it very finely or shove it through a garlic press. Fry this in two or three tablespoons of salted butter.

Drain the pasta and toss it in the garlic butter.

Serve.

Personally, I'd add chopped parsley and have a tomato or green salad with it, but Mike's never been one for gestures. It's delicious, anyway.

'The thing about this dish,' he pontificates, 'is that after she's eaten it, she knows that if she doesn't jump into bed with *you*, it's a dead cert no-one else will want to get within twenty feet of her.'

This is true. The following day my wife was early into the studio. The only person there was a lighting guy and he was about 30 yards away with his back to her. As she walked in, he said, 'Bloody hell, you're not stopping, are you?' without even turning round.

With this, we drink some red wine and then retire to the fire while the Househead grinds through her briefcase and taps away at her laptop. Does she never stop? Not, in my experience, when the washing-up is still to be done, and it was my friend who did the cooking so he's out of the frame. 'Washing-up's for Wendys,' says Mike, who can always raise a laugh down at the pub with his tuneful rendition of 'Wet Wendy's Marigolds are Blocking up the Sink' (sung to the tune of 'The Battle Hymn of the Republic'). It's just as well, I muse, that Mike's culinary creativity was as simple as it was. Macho cooks, in my experience, are not members of the 'clear up as you go' school of thought.

Before he goes, Mike starts harking back to bedtime,

bath-time and all that that domestic cliché entailed. He says he wishes he could have spent more time with his kids, but the work really had to take precedence. Not that he didn't envy me (WHAT???!!!), and it wasn't as though he thought work was the most important part of his life, but Sheila (his wife) had given up her job with Touche Ross and so he had to carry on. 'She really misses it, too. Did you know she was in line to be a very senior partner?' I did, as a matter of fact. I also knew that she'd been earning more than he had when she'd given up work to have her first baby. I also knew that Mike didn't know this, and I wasn't about to tell him. After all, we girls have to stick together, right?

'Anyway,' he says, 'it's not as if I don't see a lot of them during the holidays. Sheila leaves them with me every Saturday while she goes to see her mum. So I do get proper time with them.' I don't think it's any of my business to point out that taking them to McDonald's before settling them all down in front of the Scotland/Wales match counts as quality time. I think he's beginning to wonder why he can't raise enthusiasm for rugby among his offspring, anyway.

It will come as no surprise to you that I could tell him *that*, as well. At least I think so. Children have a pretty clear idea about both fair play and physical pain, and when they've seen some hairy All Black stomp heavily on the opposing scrum-half's ankle, or rake a few studs down the cheek of a prostrate flanker while their father explains that 'yes, it may be against both the rules and the law, but that's the way you get to WIN, see? You just hurt him a bit and he'll be a bit slower onto the ball the next time, won't he?', then you may decide that your future lies in needlework, or even housewormery.

We'd first met years before, when this Houseworm had a job and we'd faced each other in a junior school 'Father and Son' tennis competition. I'd been playing with my number two, then a doughty ten-year-old, and we both thought it was a Saturday-morning laugh. Not so Mike.

He and his eldest (well, *he* certainly) took the view that

to lose would jeopardize their futures as men, and if that meant taking a firm line with his young partner as well as with the opposition, Mike was prepared to do it. He served full-blooded belters at both of us, and when my son had the ten-year-old's temerity to whack one of them back and his son missed it, he said, 'Oh, for God's sake, Charlie!' Charlie looked mortified, but worse was to come. High lobs from us were immediately smashed back at my ten-year-old, never at me, and if the lob went to Charlie, Mike would thunder down the court yelling, 'MINE MINE MINE,' and Charlie was left to get out of the way while twelve stone of bellowing testosterone threatened to flatten him. Then there were the iffy line-calls: one of Alex's returns (off another VERY macho first serve) hummed past Charlie down the tramlines. Mike said, 'OUT,' and Charlie said, 'It was in, Dad.' Mike said, 'Don't argue with me, son. Never.' And that was that.

Once, when I was working in the restaurant bar, another 'real man' turned up. He arrived with wife and driver, and as soon as I heard the mellow, thespian boom of 'Good God, Squire, what's happened to this place?' I knew, without turning round, that we had drawn the short straw and Ollie Reed was back in town.

'A very large G&T, Squire, and a glass of white and a coke.'

Does anybody, I mean ANYBODY, call barmen or land-lords 'Squire' any more? Even in Essex?

I duly played squire for a bit, but as soon as I could slope off home for a break, I did, returning some two hours later to discover that our famous patron had just left, having first, after four more large G&Ts, taken off his shirt to display a large eagle tattooed on his back, and had then enquired of our waitress if she would like to see where the eagle has his perch.

Game for anything, our staff, and her curiosity was rewarded with the vision of (to hear her tell it) a fairly insignificant item with two talons tattooed on the end of it. When I told Mike about this he thought it was cute, and his biggest regret is that he wasn't there so he could get the great man's autograph.

Somehow we got to be friends in spite of all this, and maybe I'm exaggerating a bit with hindsight, but the world must have moved on a bit to find him sitting in front of our fire, drinking our wine (when he could be down the pub with the lads), and telling me how he envies me the benefits of housewormery and the time I can spend with my children.

'But it's the job. Anyone who leaves early enough to get home to spend time with their children is either a woman or not performing. It's OK for the women. With them it's expected.'

Me, I don't believe a word of it. The reason these half-witted Hansons are working such horrendous hours is either that they're incompetent or that they're having a ball. I suspect the latter. As a man who does it, let me tell you that night after night of homework, supper, bath-time and bed runs a pretty poor second to the appeal of a few drinks with colleagues in the Advertisers' Arms, followed by a leisurely return home to the welcome of your by now unencumbered spouse who has the drinks poured and the dinner on the table.

BUT, you can get used to it. And after a few months you begin to look back with scorn on those wasted evenings spent listening to your unmarried whiz-kid boss tell everyone how it was he who thought up your jingle that got the company a million-dollar account, and how creative early-evening brain-storming sessions in the pub really are. You know now that, for real creativity, nothing much can beat the voice you've assumed for reading *The BFG*, and your children NEVER claim that they thought it up.

'How strange the change from Macho to Minder' is a haunting little refrain, and it keeps popping into my head at the strangest times. No-one is beyond hope, not even men.

CHAPTER EIGHT

Here be Monsters

'There is no greater bugbear than a strong-willed relative
in the circle of his own connections.'

NATHANIEL HAWTHORNE

UNCLE TOBY IS THE HOUSEWORM'S ANSWER TO THE
mother-in-law joke.

I am convinced that into everyone's life there comes not
only some rain, but also some Mao-like monster, no doubt at
least half-formed by their own imagination and the monster's
mythological baggage train, but real enough for all that,
which has the power to induce in them frustration leading
to irritation leading to annoyance leading to anger leading to
blind homicidal rage, all in about two minutes thirty-seven
seconds.

It can do this even if you don't have housework and children to contend with, but add in housewormery and it can knock a minute off its time.

Where housewives have mothers-in-law who come to stay in order to drive them mad and suggest that their son is not being looked after as he would have been had the brazen trollop not got her hooks into him in the first place, I had, for a short visit that seemed like an eternity, Uncle Toby.

My wife adores her uncle, and having lost my own father at an early age the thought had crossed my mind (about twenty years ago) that this extremely successful, clever and dominant older man could just have been the sort of wiser counsel we both might need.

Like a hole in the head.

Uncle Toby, or UT (pronounced 'yute'), is a giant with a personality to match. I have met former directors of his many companies who have formed UT dining clubs where membership is open to any who know him, or have even just heard of him, but is closed to UT himself.

The reason for this is that no two people who have ever met him or even heard about him can come together without UT or UT stories immediately becoming the sole topic of conversation.

I have been at dinner parties where two of us have, as we thought, bored eight other guests rigid with the UT memoirs only to have our stories recycled elsewhere by people who've never even met the old bastard.

UT aphorisms are legion: 'The only real men you'll meet, boy, are in Welsh pubs', 'Only nancy-boys drink sherry' and 'Women were born to be beautiful and keep their mouths shut when the men are talking' and, finally, 'If you give way once, you'll give way for ever.'

This last is not, as you might expect, a warning against supine subservience but rather a precept for giving everyone you meet a good kicking as soon as possible on the chance that sheer good manners will put them in thrall to you for ever.

He should have got his knighthood for services to industry when Mrs Thatcher was PM. The fact that he didn't, simply reinforced his view that letting a woman make decisions invariably results in the wrong decisions being made. He's a Thatcherite to his boots, but survives the anomaly by believing that her policies were principally dictated by Dennis. That, in UT's view, is very much as it should be.

He is generous to a fault, and the fault is this: if your life depended on getting a pound of apples he would insist on giving you five pounds of tomatoes.

He is also the man we all know, who, if he's had a REALLY lousy day, or even if he hasn't, will go out and be rude to waiters.

This is on the not entirely spurious grounds that they want to go on working only slightly more than they want to tell him to get lost. He's always as nice as pie to proprietors, whom he fears may be unpredictably self-confident since they own the joint, but waiters, or better still young, pretty waitresses, are meat and drink to him. With them he usually starts off by saying: 'I'm ready to order, girlie . . . get me a waiter.'

Let him ask for coffee with his pudding every evening for six months, and his regular waitress may get sufficiently above herself to bring it without checking first.

'What's this?'

'Your coffee, sir.'

'If I wanted my coffee with my pudding, I'd tell you, see, so take it away!'

Within a minute, the Welsh rumble will fill the restaurant, dripping with sarcasm and accompanied by a death's head grin: 'Do you think you could become interested enough in your customers to bring me the coffee I ordered? Or is that too much trouble?'

It's got so the number-one son has developed an unerring ability to score with pretty and flustered waitresses by taking them aside, apologizing, and explaining that it's not them, it's him. Works every time.

We once lived close enough to him and Evie for him to drop in whenever he felt like it. And he nearly always felt like it. From time to time my territorial hackles rose sufficiently for me to make the not unreasonable request that he allowed us to live without supervision during the week and came to lunch when invited. This led to a fit of the sulks during which, for six weeks and more, he would not set foot on our property, invited or not.

This was by way of punishing us, you understand.

I was bathing two small people one evening, the House-head being in London, when the bathroom door opened and UT's basso profundo voice made the bathwater ripple: 'Good God, boy! How can you do that?'

I started to make some fatuous remarks along the lines of, 'Well, you run a bath, put a naked baby in it, and then this is the soap . . .' But he was already on his way downstairs.

One year, a long time ago, he came to stay. I was in charge of small people and while preparing their supper his head would appear in the kitchen. He'd sniff the air which smelt of whatever it was I was cooking, and a look of astonishment mingled with disgust would flit across his face. Then he'd say, 'Good God, what's that, boy?' and without waiting for an answer produce from behind his back whatever it was he had decided the two children OUGHT to have for supper.

Half a pound of toffees and a lump of laver bread, more likely than not.

Then: 'Boys home yet, are they?' and he'd vanish into the bowels of the house to enquire as to why sons numbers one and two were showing insufficient enthusiasm for his sea-fishing or Brecon Beacons bashing weekends.

Me? Oh, I'm still waiting for a response to my 'Oh, hi, UT!'

If I screwed my courage, small as it was, to the sticking point and put the knockers on the toffees, he would come downstairs the next day with an even bigger bag of Rowntree's finest and, leaning over the youngest and most impressionable, would say: 'I bought you these, see, but your daddy says you can't have them!'

Since my mother-in-law is a saint and my wife and my own mother are insufficiently hostile toward one another, I have no way of knowing whether UT drives me mad in the same way as an interfering mother-in-law might, but I suspect so.

I may be jealous of the affection my wife has for him, but I doubt it. What gets up my pipe is partly territorial, I guess; but mostly it's UT's energy I can't cope with.

I'm forty-seven and knackered, and he's sixty-seven and wants to explain that toffees and laver bread are vital to the diet of growing children, and indeed supply every requisite vitamin in more than the desired quantities and any doctor who says different is a second-rate tree surgeon and what's more if I tried them maybe I wouldn't be so bloody tired, boy, see?

He doesn't care what he's arguing so long as he wins, and in his book if you don't win by conviction, you can always win because the opposition gives up exhausted and leaves the field.

Even now, he and Evie occasionally come to lunch. UT lunches follow a set pattern. I prepare the usual double (*see* chapter on Cooking – for carnivores and vegetarians simultaneously) and get increasingly anxious as his arrival looms closer. By this time anything up to twelve people are cluttering up the kitchen offering to help, knocking back wine, comforting scalded children and getting in my way.

I can't open the Aga door without first moving the bloody dog, and my sense of humour has taken a sabbatical. At this point the door opens and UT walks in. Wasting no time on trivia such as 'Hullo,' he elbows his way through the throng (to where I'm standing holding a roasting tin in one hand while I stir the gravy with the other and keep the dog off the joint with my feet) and waves a bottle of wine in my face.

'Open that, will you, boy, you may as well have something worth drinking.'

This is UT for 'Gosh that smells great, it's really nice of you to invite me.'

No, really. It is.

For the next five or ten minutes, if the lunch ain't ready, and having refused all offers of a pre-lunch snort, he stands about saying things like, 'I'm sorry, boy, I thought you said one o'clock, are we early?'

One millisecond after I yell 'LUNCH EVERYBODY SIDDOWN', he disappears, taking one or more of the children with him for a 'private chat, like'. This is because he wouldn't want anyone to think he'd sat down because I'd told him to.

He's going to sit down when he's good and god-damn ready.

Polite chitchat lasts right up until I sit down after serving up. After that UT starts in: 'Well, boy, what do you think about the Lloyd's business, then?'

'Well, erm . . .' is as far as I get before he's off: 'Look, let me explain it to you, boy, just as simply as I can, see, because it's clear you need help with the clever bits . . .'

Then: 'What is this, anyway? Beef? Welsh lamb, you should be eating, see, and none of that rubbish cooking, either. Let me tell you no decent cook would use a microwave . . .'

The outcry this provokes leads him to remark cheerfully that he can explain it but only God can make us understand, given the limited size of the brains my genes have imparted to his niece's children. If the elder sons have the temerity to argue with him, he smiles like a particularly emaciated wolf in the presence of fat and tethered rabbits and remarks that if they'd inherited their mother's mind as well as her good looks there might be some hope for them, 'but in the mean time,' he confides to them secretly after lunch, 'they should stop simply parroting their father!'

The thought that these young men might disagree with him after independent thought and experience simply never crosses his mind.

Some years previously, I found an advertisement in the *Telegraph* for a book called *Nasty People and How to Deal With Them*. I surreptitiously cut it out and sent off my £12.99 or whatever.

This book changed my life!

I discovered that I was not alone; that richer and grander

and more successful men than I had encountered their own personal version of UT and been driven equally insane. Take Maxwell's henchmen, for example; but then they were at least being paid for it. Apart from the megabucks, why did they put up with it? Maxwell calling at 3 a.m. to ask what the time was? I'll tell you 'cos I know: *fear*, mostly.

None of us can believe that career success can attach itself to arrogance, prejudice and ignorance as easily as it does to Attila the Hun or Emperor Nero.

We think there must be something we're missing.

I worked for a Maxwell clone for a while, too, and I know how it feels. You keep saying to yourself that someone this successful can't be wrong. Perhaps we'd all be better off if we behaved like they do.

But in a family?

UT wouldn't have put up with it for two seconds. Evie's family were kept at arm's length, and UT's got arms to make an orang-utan envious.

What the book says is this: these are not nasty people at all . . . they are simply control freaks. They would rather do something they don't enjoy as long as it was their idea than do something they DO enjoy that someone else thought of first.

Suppose they want a cup of tea. If they arrive and say 'any chance of a cuppa?', they are in control and you (or I) make them one. If, however, you say 'have a cuppa' before they can open their mouths, you are in control and they would rather die than accept.

'No thanks, I'm just off, see?'

Pointing out that they've only just arrived will get (if my experience is anything to go by) something extremely aggressive along the lines of 'I've come to have a private chat with my niece, see? Do you have any objection?'

They hadn't, but this way they're still at the helm. Their pleasure centre is located in that bit of their psyche which quivers when they're sure they have just become the centre of someone else's world.

Ergo, the easiest way to feel good is to make someone else feel bad, 'cos that way you're in charge, right?

Ever see Maxwell make the employees squirm? Tom Bower relates how executives were flattered to have Maxwell lean across the table at a Christmas dinner until he smilingly asked them how they were going to manage after Christmas without a job or a car.

Behaving like this means you really are the centre of attention, but I don't have to put up with it and I do. Why? The book didn't say. But it did say that when I get told to open the bottle of wine and my three arms and two heads are all busy, I should remain calm and simply say, 'The corkscrew's in the second drawer down.'

'If you do this,' the book went on, 'he or she will have two options: either do it themselves, in which case YOU are in control of THEM, or drop the whole idea. Either way you win.' The book had not met UT.

HE simply turned to son number one and said, 'Come on, you do it!' . . . and of course he did.

A chip off the old block, that one.

But no . . . two people have got the better of him and I would give several years of my life to have been there on either occasion. On the first, dressed in black tie and accompanied by both wife and favourite niece, he swept up to the front of The Grosvenor House Hotel in the immaculate Rolls and, without even looking in his direction, tossed the keys to the doorman, saying, 'Don't suppose you get to park many of these, do you?'

The doorman, God bless him, didn't even blink. 'You're right, sir. Most of them have chauffeurs.'

And I am told that once, in his Chairman of the multi-national Board days, he was lunching in his regular place, where the staff had been lashed into submission by his unique mixture of giving them an extremely hard time together with extremely large tips.

On this occasion he must have encountered a new victim, a member of the waiting staff who not only refused to lie down and be walked over, but kept the Jack Dee book of witty ripostes in his apron, because when the exasperated UT finally snarled, 'Do you know who I am?', he looked him sweetly in the eye and said, 'No, sir. Why? Have you forgotten?'

UT never bothered them again.

Interfamilial warfare becomes a great deal more acute when you're a Houseworm. Mothers-in-law are unlikely to dispute the intricacies of the laws of tort with their QC daughters-in-law, but the QC has at least twenty years less experience than the old lady in the performance, or supervision, of lavatorial hygiene and laundry.

Also child-raising.

It's tough to tell the old moo she's wrong about your child's formative years when the child she formed is the one you chose to marry.

My mother-in-law gets it right. She thinks I'm a useless laundryman, an overindulgent father, a cleaner who should be reported to the Health and Hygiene Executive and a gardener of limited ability allied to a non-existent knowledge of the subject.

She likes my cooking, and she confines her judgement of my performance exclusively to saying how clever I am to cook so well, especially since I am a man, after all.

I love her to bits.

Being a Houseworm makes you really pay attention to your children. If you don't, you're dead. The big ones will have the car off you the moment you stop listening and answer 'Mmmm' to a question you didn't hear, and the smalls will push their fingers up the cat's bottom.

No high-pressure businessman (how the hell do I know when I've never been one? Well, I've met the bleeders) could be aware of the degree to which homebodies are locked into their children.

The next time I hear some father muttering about his wife 'mothering the children too much' I'll spit in his eye. A Houseworm friend of mine used to drive me berserk by constantly monitoring his two small children when I was in the middle of giving him the benefit of my profound wisdom and extreme insight in the matter of some damn thing or other; housewormery probably. But that was before I was one, see.

You cannot ever really cut yourself off from them, and unless you accept that, you will end up a twitching psychotic or in court for neglect.

It is not possible to depress the intercom button and say, 'No calls, Ms Jones,' and those who have had a lifetime being able to do just that will be flabbergasted to discover that this ain't the way things work at home.

In an office, in yours especially, you are not only in control, which becomes a habit, but you can create an environment which will allow you to do EXACTLY what you want to do. OK, right up to the time your boss barges in, but you get the idea.

Now UT has had fifty years of this, he WAS the boss, and doing what he wants is no longer a preference, it's the only activity he remains capable of.

A Houseworm has to learn to say, 'OK . . . when I've finished the laundry we'll play Princesses, OK?' This may not be being in control, but it's negotiation and a way to survive.

UT, on the other hand, adores our children and wants them all to go and spend a lot of time with him DOING WHAT HE WANTS TO DO.

'I'm going fishing next month, want to come?' demands the answer Yes or No. Yes results in enthusiasm and admiration, No results in the sulks.

The children know this, so the pressure for Yes is fairly high.

Not once has he said, though he invites them to his holiday cottage in Wales at every opportunity, 'I'm taking a long weekend, boys. Let's spend it together and what would you like to do?'

When he was staying with us I once suggested a family

outing to the Zoo, or some such. 'I'm not wasting my time driving round the country for your benefit, boy!' or words to that effect. My suggestion had been identified as a bid for control and had to be suppressed with Saddam-like ruthlessness.

And yet, and yet.

UT is sentimental, incredibly generous, frequently kind and loves deeply all the people I love, so it's hard to squash him like a bug. Actually it's bloody impossible, believe me.

With him, being in charge is an addiction that prevents him learning anything because he's the teacher, prevents him listening because he's the one doing the talking, and prevents him receiving because he's the source of all good things.

Any attempt to do something for him carries the implicitly insulting suggestion that he might need something or that he may not already have thought of everything.

The number-one son returned from a three-week period of living with a German family and on the day he got back, UT was there for lunch. UT's experience of Germany amounts to three days in the smartest hotel in Frankfurt.

'Well, boy, how was it? Did you learn about the Germans? Did you realize that the chief characteristic of the German people is that they are . . . just listen, boy, you might learn something.'

Every time the son showed any sign of disagreement with the lunch-length lecture that followed he was told that it was clear he had no insight and clearly no interest in finding out, twin failings that a little close attention to UT would remedy where three weeks' first-hand experience had clearly failed.

Are you out there, UT? No hard feelings, I just thought you might like to know that you've been pretty central to this Houseworm's life for quite a while.

CHAPTER NINE

Cave Canem

'The best thing about animals is that they don't talk much.'

THORNTON WILDER

THE REASON PEOPLE KEEP DOGS IS THAT THEY ARE THE sort who need to ensure that when they get home something, at least, is pleased to see them.

What this says about their sense of self-worth I leave the world to judge, but to desire the approval of the only carnivorous mammal known to prefer catshit to Kennomeat is pretty peculiar.

Dogs are awful. We have one and I know.

The only practical use anyone can find for a dog is, in the absence of a weather-vane, to find out which way the wind's blowing. Simply take the dog for a walk, and wherever it chooses to perform will be directly upwind of you. It's uncanny, unpleasant, but accurate. Me, I'd rather not know.

Now things could have turned out differently and I could have been a successful actor lounging about on colour supplement weekends, sporting plaid shirt, corduroys and Labrador for the benefit of my adoring public, and, in common with most career-dominated 'dog-lovers', I'd have made damn sure the spouse looked after the dog.

Before we got married, on one of the many weekends I spent with Penny's parents, their Labrador was pregnant. My about-to-be-wife's father was an enthusiastic dog owner who followed this spouse/dog rule to the letter. His wife, who couldn't abide the brute, was expected to feed, water and clear up after this soppy animal and in return she (the bitch, not the wife) cringed, slobbered and drooled with enthusiasm at the feet of he who never did a thing for her.

One night she was delivered of six puppies, and guess who the midwife was?

Yup, me.

All the dog-lovers were fast asleep and this animal was in a serious mess. My compassion was rewarded by being taken as incontrovertible proof that I really loved dogs, in spite of my protests, and I had to become extremely firm to avoid being given one of the puppies.

I still think their lack of involvement demonstrates equally clearly that none of them could give a toss about the dog at any time other than when it's doing that 'Gosh, aren't you wonderful (wag, wag, slobber, fart) to come home to little me who simply lives for your every glance' garbage.

When dogs are not being sick on the carpet, they are dumping on the lawn. When they are not dumping on the lawn they are letting go long, languorous farts from beneath the dining table during dinner. When they stop farting they start to copulate with the bare leg of your most important female dinner guest, and when that's done they'll push a wet, cold nose into her crotch and start blowing slobber-bubbles.

When that's done, and the bugger's given the contents of the dishwasher the usual revolting pre-wash, it's time to go back to being sick on the carpet.

This is what dogs do. Don't give me that stuff about how noble they look with their ears blowing in the wind. They'd look just as noble, and be a lot less messy, if you had them stuffed and wheeled them into the most picturesque position outside the french windows.

If you're one of those *Daily Telegraph*-reading pillars of the Kennel Club, please don't bother to become apoplectic. It won't make me like dogs, and it won't change the nature of the beasts. Both they, and you, will still be revolting.

If, however, you want to understand your enemy (me), then all you have to do is undertake to be entirely responsible for a newly acquired (by someone other than yourself, that is) puppy, and simultaneously take on the labours of the average Houseworm.

I defy you to regard with equanimity, let alone sympathy and affection, the trail of wet-puppy paw-prints that lead with grim determination across the high gloss of your just-polished floor, to the steaming heap of regurgitated cow-pat on your newly hoovered Axminster.

If you are into those dog-training manuals you will be telling yourself that this is not the dog's fault, it is yours; that in some way you have failed to anticipate its needs and steer its psyche in a mutually acceptable direction. Bollocks!

What you will be thinking, should you ever get into this position, is that you want the dog dead.

Better still, you want to strangle it, slowly, with your bare hands, and when it's dead you want to kick its head in.

Trust me on this; really.

Cats, on the other hand, are equally equipped to ruin the best-laid plans of the hygienic Houseworm, but at least they are a) a sort of living sculpture, b) individually discriminating and c) couldn't give a Sunday-afternoon toss whether you live or die.

I used to be a cat-lover, but a year or so of swinging my

bare feet out of bed and into the cat-sick at six-thirty has just about done for that.

The other thing is gall-bladders.

How do they know? We have three semi-Siamese and two tortoiseshell mogs, none of whom have any trouble consuming one and a half pounds of freshly ambushed grey squirrel, including fur, tail, paws and head, but who, with the skill of a Harley Street surgeon, invariably extract the gall-bladder and leave it somewhere as a surprise; usually in one of my slippers, or camouflaged in the pattern on the Chinese rug, where a distant popping noise beneath my feet is the only indication that the rug has now lost what little value it had.

Quite a small cat can, I have discovered, not only kill a fully grown buck rabbit, but can transport it, as if by magic, up onto the kitchen roof via a window ledge, and from there across the tiles and in through the number-one son's bedroom window where it will disembowel it against the wall right under the head of the bed.

This ensures that the blood gets straight onto the fitted carpet, every other square inch being covered in clothes, books, papers and childhood treasures dating back to the Precambrian.

This son is also the only person who can be guaranteed a) not to wake up during the butchery and b) not to notice the smell until all hope of getting the stain out of the carpet has vanished.

We have always had some sort of Siamese presence in our lives, which probably accounts for my unwonted sentimentality about the vicious brutes. In the dim and rosy past where our only living responsibilities were two Siamese cats called Damn and Blast, we used to load them up in our Volkswagen camper and head out of London every weekend.

Wherever we stopped, from the New Forest to a Welsh beach, we'd simply open the sliding door and they'd slope off into the night. Once we had to rescue them from a cliff ledge in Cornwall where they'd been prospecting among a colony of herring gulls who took a markedly dim view of their activities and had them pinned down in abject terror while the birds dived, screaming, to within inches of their little pointed ears.

One night we stopped in a remote bit of Ashdown Forest, let the cats out and went to sleep. I was woken in the early-summer dawn by the unmistakable low humming growl of a Siamese cat disputing ownership of some still-warm corpse with a sibling. Lifting the top of our double sleeping-bag, I looked down to see two small cats snarling at each other from either side of my still-sleeping wife's naked stomach, on which lay the bleeding carcase of a young rabbit. Much merriment ensued, not all of it shared by either the wife, who refused to lie still after my giggles woke her, or the cats, who resented having their breakfast slung out of the camper with shrieks of outrage.

Perhaps that accounts for the vegetarianism.

Cats are retromingent, a wonderful name for the ability to pee backwards, which allows them to back up on anything, wiggle their backsides, and cover it with a foul-smelling yellow stain that only rubber gloves, Flash, hot water and disinfectant can remove, and even then the memory (and more) lingers on.

Our mistake was to take in the two abandoned tortoiseshell kittens when the existing three semi-Siameses were getting on a bit and set in their ways. One of them had been a tom until I had him dealt with to stop the spraying, which was beginning to be detectable downwind for a considerable distance.

The day I loaded him into a basket to take him to the vet, he knew exactly what was going on. Emitting a bass growl of ear-splitting intensity, he backed up against the wire of the cat basket, and sprayed copiously all over the upholstery of my company Renault. It took me eight months to get rid of that car, and I finally sold it because the salesman only asked me if it was mechanically sound before he agreed to take it as a part exchange. Once he got in, his face took on the unmistakable look of a man who knows he's been done, and by an amateur at that. He wound down the window; quite quickly, I thought.

'Can I tell you something?' he asked. 'Not even Feu d'Orange can get the smell of cat's pee out of cheap velour.'

'I know,' I said. 'It's been there eight months and I've tried everything.'

'Do me a favour,' he said. 'Next time you want a new car, go somewhere else.'

As for the cat, nobody ever said having your nuts off affected your ability to retrominge. It may be a bit less pungent these days, but peeing all over the side of the microwave, into the food processor and all over the glasses in the glass cupboard is in a league of its own when it comes to expressing disapproval of two new cats being taken into what the freeholders consider their territory.

Then there are horses. Horses are a lot better than dogs or cats insofar as they don't actually dump on the duvet. However, it is my experience that those who wish to ride horses are not invariably those who wish to spend every last minute looking after them. 'Why,' these people like to ask themselves, 'should I be expected to muck out, rub down and hoof-pick when God in his wisdom created the Houseworm, who has sod all to do all day and ought to be glad of the exercise?'

We had two horses for a time, and when the wife was busy with her Househead's breadwinning activities and the second son was away at school (something that seemed to date from the day we finally gave in to his desire for a horse), then the Houseworm's responsibilities were extended to include hay-and-water distribution, mucking out, manure-pile maintenance and being there to pay the farrier £60 a month and the vet whatever number he first thought of.

Those who have never tried it may be unaware of the intricacies of equestrian ownership and the horse-person's responsibilities *vis-à-vis* the local economy, and I confess that where I came from a horse lived in a field until whoever wanted to be bothered caught it, stuck a bridle and maybe a saddle on it, and rode off into the sunset. Not, you will be unsurprised to learn, so.

The new horse-owner is obliged to purchase lengthy manuals dedicated to the proposition that there's one born every minute, and the fact that you've got a horse means you must be both rich and stupid.

Back from Simone's Super Saddlery would come the wife, together with a travel rug (for each horse), a string vest (ditto) and something called a New Zealand which is the equine equivalent of a Barbour jacket, and the animal wouldn't be seen dead in anything else, my dear.

Also hoof oil, worming tubes, fly screens, leg and tail bandages and for all I know equine Tampax and Wash & Go shampoo.

The reason the horses needed all this stuff, it was explained to me as though to a half-wit, was that Simone (she of the Super Saddlery) said so.

I can't for the life of me think why, especially since she turns out to be none other than the author of the horse handbook that started all this. Still, they say the economy's picking up, and I, for one, know why.

Horses are really quite seriously stupid. If they find themselves in a field full of green, lush grass, they will eat until they get blown up like a football and their legs get inflamed from all the extra weight. So what the Houseworm has to do is set up a system of electric fencing to keep the imbeciles from committing suicide through gluttony.

They will also eat ragwort which will kill them, rhododendrons which will not do them any good, and if you don't fence it off they'll fall in the river.

Once the electric fence is in place they lean on it, get a belt, panic, and, instead of moving away, they gallop through the blasted thing, tearing it all up and knackering the power source. Then they get back to committing suicide by gluttony.

When they are not doing this they are rubbing their backsides against a bit of post and rail that some cretin (yeah, yeah) hasn't secured properly so that the top rail falls out and they can step over onto the newly seeded and exquisitely rolled lawn and eat the contents of the herbaceous border. When challenged, they can then get into an absolute tizzy and gallop some hoof-prints 10 inches across and 6 inches deep into said lawn because their tiny brains have failed to retain the location of the hole in the fence they got out by.

This doesn't ultimately matter since at full gallop your average cob can make a perfectly adequate hole to get back in by, just about anywhere it feels like it.

As I spend the next three weeks trying to fill the holes in both the fence and the lawn, I begin to reflect that among the horse-lovers, as among the dog-lovers, this will probably all turn out to have been my fault.

There are, of course, smaller pets.

The first of the long trail of small furry friends acquired as pets by our children was a hamster called Arrow who lasted about a week. The number-one son, aged four, conned us into this responsibility by the usual method of blinking back tears, while saying, 'Oh, please can I have him? Please? Please?' in a piteous voice, and vowing that he would dedicate the rest of his waking life to looking after his new friend's every need.

On day six of the rest of his life, he left the door of its cage open (have you noticed how the animal costs 60p while the cage alone sets you back thirty quid?), and Arrow was out of there as if he had a name to live up to. After an hour and a half of fruitless searching accompanied by a good deal of wailing, howling and gnashing of teeth, son number one threw himself dramatically onto his bed declaring that he didn't want to live without his oppo.

This dramatic gesture was heightened by the fact that his bed at the time was a mattress on a legless divan base and that as he landed, there came from under it a single, muffled and definitely terminal squeak.

So that was Arrow.

If it hadn't suffered death by falling owner, I'd probably still be looking after it. I seem to have inherited just about every other living thing originally acquired at great emotional expense by our children, who without exception lost interest within two weeks or, in any case involving Rosie, within two hours.

Two weeks if you're lucky, but sure as God made little green apples, any time after that, if you mention the name Fluffy, or Silky, or Snowy, or whatever the hell, the child will say, 'Huh? Wha'? I'm watching *Neighbours*, Dad!'

Long before this you will have discovered that gerbils require add-ons like wheels, tunnels, tubes and mirrors, all of which presumably occur naturally in the African desert, but now need to come in injection-moulded plastic from the pet shop and NOT out of the drawer-full of the ruddy things you've had ever since good old Patch, or Trixie, or Clemmie, or whatever it was called, passed away.

Or *was* passed away; by the dog, I seem to remember. He had the runs for a week.

So what happens is that YOU get lumbered. There's nothing quite like the sight of a forty-seven-year-old man wandering up the garden whispering sweet nothings into the ear of a guinea-pig, or finding himself spending what John Major would call a not inconsiderable part of his day holding conversations with the cats. Or even, God forbid, the dog.

The only good thing about having cats, in fact, is that by their very nature they are inclined to curb the rodent population; both feral and, I'm glad to say, domestic. This can occasionally be upsetting, as when Penny stepped naked from the shower to see the guinea-pig's face staring up at her from the middle of the bathroom floor.

Just the face, that is.

The rest of the guinea-pig was in the cat.

Come to think of it, I never did find that gall-bladder.

We've had birds, too, that have fallen to the Houseworm's

lot. It was chickens for eggs that started it, but then we get all sentimental and vegetarian when the time comes to top them all, make really good chicken soup and get in some more point-of-lay birds, so we end up with four scraggy old numbers who have survived both old age and the fox and who lay about one egg a fortnight.

And that's between them.

This does not mean they don't eat the same amount as they ever did when there were twelve of them. The two geese are equally useless but a good deal more intimidating. There being no gander means that when they come into lay in the spring the eggs are unfertilized.

This does not stop these two middle-aged ladies setting up home together and defending to the death an ever-expanding number of non-hatching eggs. Hissing, spitting and biting, they'll have the wellies off anyone trying to muscle in on their family.

Once the eggs are well and truly addled, the two dykes get bored with the game and break them, leaving a smell that even the chickens find offensive. More mucking out for the Houseworm.

For her fortieth birthday I bought the Househead a white dovecote and a pair of white fan-tail pigeons and a pair of the most elegant Java doves. It was necessary to keep these birds, purchased in the North of England, shut into the dovecote for six weeks while they got used to their new home. This meant daily feeding and watering and finally the day came when they could all take up their new jobs of flying spectacularly about making aerial arabesques above our happy home to the universal envy and admiration of the neighbours.

I opened the wire front to the Java doves' apartment and the two of them came out over my head at Mach 7, and by the time I'd fallen off my ladder and got up again they were being welcomed back to their loft in Littlewick on t'Moor and prepared for sale to the next Southern sucker to show up. The white fan-tails, however, stuck around.

Not, of course, in the expensive and purpose-built dovecote so thoughtfully provided, but under the eaves of the house, from where their fluttering wings set off the security light sensors throughout the night (they do it deliberately – as far as they're concerned the security lights are their own personal central-heating system) and their droppings leave charcoal-grey smear marks all down the white walls before forming a pile outside the french windows that the dog can roll in if he's not hungry.

The last feathered item on this Houseworm's list of responsibilities is Joe's cockatiel. A standard grey-and-white semi-parrot with yellow cheeks and crest, it has been provided with a cage of great splendour and magnificence on, rather than in, which it sits each night to sleep.

As soon as it's light it flies across the room to perch on the back of an armchair in front of a full-length mirror where it holds interminable and frequently abusive discussions with its own reflection and shows its contempt for its mirror-image by cacking all over the armchair's upholstery and the surrounding floor. Getting cockatiel cack off parquet is only marginally easier than getting blood out of either carpets or, for that matter, stones.

The cockatiel is extremely picky about whose shoulder it is prepared to perch on, and, as a result, I feel flattered that while I'm writing it might deign to fly across and land on my head.

It then wanders down my arm before stamping unerringly on the word-processor's delete key.

It also perches on my shoulder by my ear, and if I have failed to shave my whole face very closely, it reaches across, seizes one bristle in its beak, and then uses the whole of its weight to try and pull it out. This hurts like hell, and my bellow of rage usually induces the bird to scream back and cack on my shoulder.

This, I can't help thinking, is where the Houseworm came in. The Houseworm gets dumped on by EVERYBODY.

CHAPTER TEN

More Muck than Magic

'A garden is a loathesome thing, God wot!'

(with apologies to) THOMAS EDWARD BROWN

BY MAY OF THE MAJOR YEAR, JUST AS I'M BEGINNING TO think I can handle this, a new factor slots itself into the equation. As soon as the spring temperature hits six degrees Celsius I'm in trouble.

This is the temperature at which grass starts to grow, and means that from now on, throughout the summer, not one moment will be my own. Lawns don't just lie there and look reproachfully at you, you know. They also shop you to your guests.

I have been burdened, since birth, with a number of South African relatives, all of whom, at one time or another, turn up here in order that I may proudly show them just how good the home-town boy has made.

They usually show up in twos. This is so that having been shown their bedroom and seen the veg. garden on their way in, one of them can walk into the sitting-room, look out of the french windows at the pristine lawn and yell out, 'Hey, man, come an' take a look . . . they've got more grazing out here!'

It's all God's fault. No, listen: 'And the Lord God took the man, and put him into the Garden of Eden to dress it and keep it.'

Two things: if it was the Garden of Eden why did it need to be dressed and kept? If I ever make it to Paradise, am I going to be lumbered with the washing-up?

And I now know why Adam was so keen on the apple. He figured getting into trouble was a lot better than an eternity with the celestial Fisons, especially since he could blame the whole sorry mess on a woman. He was right, too.

Now that distance, and poverty, lend some enchantment to the view, I look back, with a sort of horrible nostalgia, on those extravagant days when we had 'help' in the garden from one or other of the clearly demented people that Care in the Community had ensured took up our offers of employment.

Even Jacko.

Jacko was interviewed for the job with one wife, but when he turned up he'd got a different one. Well, you don't like to ask, do you? On his first morning we went round the garden together to sort of establish a game plan. My idea was that he would do the maintenance. You know, weeding, lawns, hedges and veges, and that each year we'd have a project, like a new bed, or a pond, or something that would get both of us at it and relieve the monotony for him.

He had a different idea.

His was that he would talk and I would listen, and then every now and again I would stop listening long enough to get him a cup of coffee or a spot of lunch, "cos the missis don't 'old with lunch, see?'

A plantsman he wasn't.

'What are we going to do about that?' I asked, pointing to a smallish bed with lots of ground-covering greenery.

'Aaah, well,' said Jacko. 'That's just the stuff, that is. We 'ad that down where I was in Sussex about fifteen year ago now. Lovely it was. Its proper name's just slipped my memory. *Sax* . . . something in Latin. Likes a good bit of lime, that does, and no mistake. Come the winter I'll transfer some from there to the front of the house. It ain't difficult to grow. Not if you know what you're doin', it ain't.'

He was right about that, anyway. It was ground elder.

Jacko set up home for himself in the tractor shed. Kettle, tin tray, bottle of milk, instant coffee, sugar, two mugs ('One for visitors?' I asked myself) and the *Daily Star*.

'What,' I was foolish enough to quip, one day when I found him deep in coffee and page three at ten fifteen, 'no chocolate Hob-Nobs?'

'Naah, I 'aven't. Thanks very much, guv, you're a gemmun.'

At moments like these he always ensured that the tractor, or the mower, or the strimmer was either jacked up with its wheels off or lying in pieces all over the floor. If I surprised him mid coffee-break (impossible not to do provided you dropped in between 9 a.m. and 5 p.m.), he would immediately say: 'Oh, hullo, guv, I'm glad you come in. I got a problem with this fuel pump/rocker cover/con-rod or oil filter.' (Perm any three from twelve, he'd sussed out at the interview that I couldn't tell a half-shaft from a Holloway Road Haberdashers.)

It's in one of those insidious works of dramatic fiction, like *The Servant* or *The Creeper*, that the character who's supposed to be in charge gradually discovers that he ain't, the help is, and that there's nothing he can do about it.

The only fiction I can detect in these triumphs of the art

of holding the mirror up to nature is that there's nothing gradual about it.

You know how two dogs instinctively know who's tougher, and the wetty immediately goes through a laborious body-language ritual involving rolling over, tail wagging and every piece of revoltingly submissive behaviour in the hopes of avoiding getting his canine butt kicked?

Well, the tough dog never has to actually demonstrate his superior powers, both dogs just *know*.

It's the same with Jacko.

That's how he got the job. He knew I was a walk-over at the interview, and I immediately knew that he was in charge. Such knowledge, such experience; where had this horticultural Margaret Thatcher *been* all my life? There was nothing, I instantly realized, that he didn't know and couldn't do, and every time in the future that I felt like getting out in my own garden for a bit of outdoors, he would be there to aid and instruct.

Weeds, unmown lawns, slugs, overgrown paths and nettle beds set off by evidence of the efficiency of the dog's digestive tract would all be things of the past.

To convince me of this he didn't actually DO or SAY anything at all.

He just agreed with me a lot, explained that getting to grips with our garden was all he ever wanted to do with his life, and if we were both busy he was very happy to work unsupervised as he'd had a lot of supervision (interference, he called it) at his last place.

As far as I could subsequently ascertain, his last place had been Rampton.

But blinded by body-language and the self-confidence that could only have come from Jacko's absolute knowledge that I was a berk and his secret identity was Lord Throng of Alpha Centauri disguised as a gardener only until the invasion, we took him on.

He lasted about three months. During this time, having

the use of our car, he would discover from time to time that he needed a particular bolt or something.

Leaping behind the wheel, he would set off, not for our local engineering shop, but ('it's 'ALF THE PRICE, GUV') for a distant DIY hypermarket. After a round trip of twenty miles he would return, and after carefully fitting his prize to whatever bit of garden machinery he was currently engaged upon transforming into a Centaurian battle-blaster, he would discover that he needed another, identical, bolt.

We would stand, silently, and watch the car leave. Our fuel account would have sniggered at the Gross National Product of most Central American republics.

Now that he's gone, I miss him.

The garden machinery now displays all the boring, predictable characteristics of things that actually work, and the greenhouse is full of tomatoes, instead of Jacko's lovingly nurtured collection of nettles, docks and plantain.

'You don't wanna pull them up, guv . . . it's them as keeps the whitefly away.'

I didn't fire him. Could the third corporal from the left have fired Custer? He came in one day and said 'e didn't want to let us down, like, but gardening didn't agree wiv 'im on account of his fingernails. 'is missis said she didn't 'old wiv 'em and he was packin' it in tomorrow and could he 'ave 'is money now? And the extra week in lieu of notice, since he 'adn't given us any? Ta, guv.

No, really, he did.

The machinery may work now, but the drawback is that I have to as well, and most machines, but especially those with the ability to inflict serious injury, usually do so on me.

In 1976, after all the elm trees died, I was retained by my father-in-law to fell a line of dead trees in one of his fields. My companion in this venture was one Malcolm Stoddard, an actor very much more frequently in work than I, who also knew a bit about the business of tree-felling, logging, and not using chain-saws on yourself in such a way as to ensure that all future acting engagements come through Hammer Films.

After the first morning had seen the successful dropping, in more or less the right direction, of two large trees, we stopped for a well-earned lunch.

Being my father-in-law's house, the lunch naturally included a few beers beforehand and a few glasses of red with the sausages. Not for Malcolm, of course, who is both careful *and* vegetarian.

Brimming with *bonhomie* and singing the 'I'm a Lumber-jack and I'm OK' song from Monty Python, I returned to set about the elms with renewed enthusiasm. In thirty seconds I'd put the chain-saw through my leg. It was lucky, I thought hysterically at the time, that there was a bone in my shin, because that's what stopped the whizzing chain after it went through my calf muscle.

Malcolm, who had secretly suspected I was about to make an idiot of myself, got me in the Land-rover and off to casualty as if he'd been trained as a paramedic as well.

We stopped at the front door of the house, with me holding my leg together in the passenger seat, long enough to inform wives and mothers-in-law that there was 'nothing to worry about, but James has had a minor accident with a chain-saw and we're just popping off to hospital for a check-up.'

Malcolm had a natural talent for pouring oil on troubled waters and then setting fire to it.

Years later, after my damascene revelation that the reason Malcolm could earn a living as an actor was that he was a very good one and the reason I couldn't was . . . OK, OK already.

So I went to Business School courtesy of the grateful taxpayers, and there I met a management psychologist who gave us one of those tests that are supposed to provide you with an employee's aptitude for a particular job. It tests intelligence, co-ordination and some characteristics I wouldn't have believed possible. The lady psychologist looked at our test results and then looked at us.

'Which of you is Mr Leith?'

'Huh?'

'Would you mind telling me how many serious injuries you have suffered in your life?'

'What do you mean by serious?'

'How about anything that's led to permanent scarring excluding operations?'

I goggled at her and counted scars.

'Nine.'

The gasps of astonishment this provoked amongst my classmates was a revelation to me.

Doesn't everyone collect a few scars in thirty years? The psychologist asked the class (there were about twenty of us, all post-graduates with an average age of about twenty-eight) if anyone else had had more injuries.

The same number?

Eight?

Seven?

Six?

The first hand went up at three.

'You see?' she said smugly. 'Your psychological profile showed the highest score for being accident-prone that I or my colleagues have ever seen. If you worked for me, you would not be permitted to operate machinery, particularly cutting machinery.'

Just goes to show what rubbish these psychologists come up with. I mean, look at me. I'm a Houseworm and gardener. Scissors, cook's knives, barding needles, hot plates, food processors, flail mowers, chain-saws, rotary mowers and brushcutters are my stock-in-trade.

My wife says it's only a matter of time.

Gardening is the worst of the unremitting tasks that confront the Houseworm.

Not excluding childcare.

It has been described as 'the purest of pleasures' by people who ought to know better or whose sensory deprivations have been such that they should experiment as soon as possible with some of the other pleasures available on the open market.

No pleasure can be gained from an activity that requires the performer to keep running, like the Red Queen, simply to remain in the same place.

Dedicate five years of your life to the creation of a garden and settle back to enjoy it. Within slightly less than the time it takes to pour yourself a celebratory glass of something to accompany you to the hammock and the latest copy of *Country Life*, the lawn will need mowing, the border need weeding, the roses need pruning, the lilies need staking, the blackfly need spraying, the creeper need tying, the hedge need trimming and Mother Nature, the bitch, will be back in charge.

We once sold a house to a landscape gardener.

The house, the famous one-up, one-down cottage, had a small, pretty garden with an apple tree, and we wondered what a man whose career was built on horticultural imagination would do with it.

'You kidding? I'm going to concrete the whole thing over and cover it in white pebbles with a fountain in the middle, and once a year I'll soak it in Pathclear and rake patterns in the pebbles. Dashed cunning the Japanese.'

A man of infinite vision.

My brother-in-law likes lawns. This is because he employs a great many people to tend them.

The wise Houseworm refrains from getting delusions of adequacy and will confine his lawn-tending to applying the mower and nothing else.

After several years of this the traditional grass lawn will have become the far more avant-garde 'moss', decorated with dark-green circles of plantains and sparkling with white daisies and yellow dandelions. Why, in the name of all that's wonderful, do you want GRASS? It only grows.

Moss has the advantage of hardly ever needing to be cut and it's green as well. For a deeper colour, try clover, or allow the dark-green clover to form great swathes through the moss, thereby creating a dappled effect, punctuated by divots where the sons practise their 8 irons under The Editor's benign tutelage.

You want to grow your own vegetables? Hah! Lemme tell you something, pal.

Next time you get the urge to join the good lifers, try this.

Hire a Rolls Royce, complete with chauffeur, for two days. Have this ensemble transport you to London and check into the Dorchester. Take in a play followed by dinner at Le Gavroche or Chez Nico. After a leisurely breakfast have the chauffeur transfer you to Harrods where you may spend, if you wish, several hours selecting the finest fruit and vegetables from among the mouth-watering displays in the food-hall, and then, pausing only to consume an extravagant lunch at Mosimann's, have the driver convey you home with your booty.

This, I assure you, is an infinitely cheaper way of acquiring veg than attempting to grow the bloody things yourself.

The thing about Mother Nature, the bitch, is that she gets your juices going by sending you, in the depths of winter, those seed catalogues from Thompson and Morgan or Suttons or Marshalls, all filled with colour pictures of 380 different varieties of tomato, and you fall for it.

You send off an order for seeds that includes things like vegetable spaghetti and asparagus peas and several other former weeds that the marketing men have transformed into the fashionable new cuisine vegetarienne. You forgo holidays, golf and weekends to till, rake, sow, water, transplant and weed more seedlings than you believe could possibly have originated in your modest order, and then the slugs appear and eat them all.

By this time perennial foodstuffs like berries and asparagus are providing a welcome change for woodlice, beetles, mice, squirrels, rabbits, deer and a colony of blackfly that got bored with 'Life with the Lupins'.

Ma Nature, the bitch, then waits, like UT, until you're

dying for a crisp spring lettuce or a creamy new potato and then, all at once, she ensures that your garden is overrun with both just as the prohibitive prices in the shops come rocketing down to the point where you are being paid to take 'em away.

'Aah,' I hear Clay Jones saying, 'that's why you 'ave a green'ouse. You can bring 'em on a bit, then, and it'll be lovely!'

I don't know where he gets it all from, I really don't.

In my experience it takes four hours to fill a very small greenhouse with trays of newly sown seed, the odd pot of something or other and the vine that took seven years to produce any grapes and those immediately succumbed to mildew.

It then takes another twenty minutes a day to water them. It's then another four-hour job to prick out, then another four to pot on or plant out and then it takes no time at all for the spring sunshine to ensure that whatever's in the greenhouse dies of thirst while whatever isn't dies of frost.

Doesn't this Jones bloke have work to do? I thought all this gardening stuff was supposed to be a hobby.

Farmers get discouraged by having to do a job that involves trying to second-guess God.

Who, in their right mind, wants to do it during their time off? OK, nobody in their right mind, but then I'm a Houseworm and I don't get any time off.

We have a kitchen garden complete with potting shed containing earthenware pots packed in their original 1850 straw. It's a shame not to use it, thought I, egged on by the BBC's *Victorian Kitchen Garden*, and every year I fall for the catalogues and go through the whole horrible ritual, but each year I learn a little and do less.

My goal is to mark the summer by filling the greenhouse with basil plants and, by constant cropping, to ensure a supply of pesto throughout the year. It's pesto, not Ray Bradbury's dandelion wine, that encapsulates all the smells and tastes of summer, and when I've reduced my gardening to the establishment of one gigantic basil crop I shall have achieved the highest state of horticultural development.

CHAPTER ELEVEN

Pasta Master

'Kissing don't last. Cookery do!'

GEORGE MEREDITH

I HAVE PREVIOUSLY TOUCHED ON SUCH ERUDITE CULI-
nary matters as the pickiness of vegetarians who should know
better, the Yuk Factor in children of any age, from nine
months to nineteen years, and the parental psychosis that
denies the nutritional benefits of anything labelled 'place in
Microwave for three minutes on full power and serve'.

It is a truth universally acknowledged that a man in
possession of an ability to cook, together with a supply
of white truffles and a bottle of extra virgin olive oil (cold-
pressed by Tuscan peasants at midnight beneath the towers
of San Gimigniano), must be in search of impressionable
dinner guests.

He is not intending to devote his culinary expertise to the production of spaghetti and tomato sauce sandwiches, which comestibles form the thrice-daily diet of my younger children.

Even in the days before housewormery I was happy to cook. Laden with expensive ingredients, I would enter the kitchen with the bravura air of an ace toreador about to despatch several bulls, all of which he knows are doped to the eyeballs, and within three hours the kitchen would be reduced to a flour-encrusted, oil-smeared, smoke-filled set for Gogol's *Lower Depths*; the children would be in tears because 'Daddy yelled at me and I didn't DO anything', the wife would have offered to help and would now not be speaking to me, and the face of a three-star Michelin chef on the cover of his £25 hardback recipe collection entitled *Ma Cuisine Magnifique* would be being rained on in its resting place in the flower-bed outside the kitchen window.

Then we would go to the pub.

Cooking, as any Houseworm knows, is not about dinner parties. It is about stuffing sufficient nutrients in as palatable a form as possible down the necks of spouse and offspring so that they don't end up making medical history as the first British cases of kwashiorkor.

Only those who are not responsible for this aspect of parenthood and conjugal bliss think it would be great to 'get in the kitchen, whip up a little something and invite the Blenkinsops over'.

I did it once.

Just once.

We were at a drinks party and, in the spirit that only eight glasses of BYOB in rapid succession can induce, I heard myself say, 'Why don't you all come back to us for supper? It's no trouble, is it, darling?'

The spouse, who, I had momentarily forgotten, was due to catch a flight to Manchester at 6.30 a.m., managed to smile sweetly and sink a three-inch heel into my instep while simultaneously saying, 'What do you mean US, white man?' without moving her lips.

Happily anaesthetized, I grinned confidently back and assured her that she could, if she wished, retire to bed and listen enviously to the sounds of merrymaking interspersed with astonished cries of praise for her husband's cooking that would filter sweetly up the stairs.

'Planning,' I said, as she picked up her coat. 'Tha's all you need. S'easy p'vided you plan ahead.'

'Men,' I continued, as she plucked the car keys from my inert fingers, 'men do planning. Tha's what men do. You watch.'

She drove us sweetly home, put the car in the garage, unlocked the back door, turned on the lights and waited for me to get up from among the milk bottles thoughtfully left on the step outside.

'Look,' I said. 'S'easy,' I said. 'I'll do pasta . . . three different sauces, too. 'Cos for why? 'Cos we got the EQUIP-MENT, tha's why. Planning, see? S'easy, no trouble. You can watch, 'few like, mmmh?'

She didn't seem to be paying attention. She didn't seem to want to watch, either.

'They'll be here in fifteen minutes,' she said. 'Good night.' And she went upstairs to bed.

One of the greatest culinary marvels of the twentieth century is a thing called a Thermomix. This is a blender that cooks or a cooker that blends, and it's triffic. You can put in flour, milk, butter, bay-leaf, whole pepper corns, salt and a pinch of mustard and in ten minutes you've got white sauce; hot, smooth, shiny and ready to go. Chuck in a few lumps of cheddar, whizz, and, hey presto, cheese sauce from white sauce in five seconds. This was my secret weapon. Boy, was I going to show her. 'Planning, see. Tha's all you need. Big saucepan a' pasta, full of boiling water; li'l oil stop it sticking together, salt; all done. Three sauces easy. Cheese sauce first, mushroom sauce second, tomato sauce third. Dark colours last, huh? Saves washing the Thermomix out between. Clever, hey? 'mean am I genius or what? Watch this an' weep, woman.'

A thought.

These twenty-odd revellers are going to need booze.

Better to open the wine first, my diamond-sharp intellect suggests, then they can keep out of my way in the sitting-room while I prepare to astound and amaze. Can't find the corkscrew.

While looking for it, the water for the pasta boils over.

The trouble with putting oil in the water is that oil floats on water (ask anyone who was on the *Torrey Canyon* or the *Exxon Valdez*) so when it boils over the oil's on top and comes out first all over the hotplate of the Aga and very soon smells horrible, not to mention producing a thickish smoke, making breathing difficult which means I have to open all the windows and then clear up, wipe hotplate, burn my thumb, hold thumb under cold water, find plaster that doesn't stick to wet thumb and decide bugger it before putting on a new pan of water, more oil, salt and then go back to looking for the corkscrew.

'S funny how quick fifteen minutes goes, innit?'

Doorbell rings at front just as revellers who know we always come in the back fall over the milk bottles.

One reveller carries Swiss army knife with corkscrew so delegate booze and indicate direction of sitting-room. 'Need help? Funny smell in here. Got a problem? What we having? I'm starving. Any beer? Where's the crisps then? What's all this smoke?' guaranteed to irritate.

'Bog off,' I graciously respond. 'Go'n sit inna sitting-room and don't bug me. Food in ten minutes.'

By now the pasta is cooking and the white sauce is grinding away and since there's a bottle of wine open, I decide that the Keith Floyd of Dorking needs a drink. After a short reverie to contemplate the precision of my planning, I throw in three large lumps of cheddar.

('Don' cut 'em small! Machine's 'smazing. Grind up anything. Watch.')

The trouble with throwing largish lumps of solids into a bowl of very hot semi-solid white sauce in which the Thermomix blades are whizzing about at turbo-speed is that their first effect is to propel said lumps, with hot sauce adhering, UP and OUT.

Results can best be observed from the door of the kitchen by close friends whose concern for the welfare of the Keith Floyd of Dorking is entirely swamped by hysteria at the sight of him trying to get burning hot lumps of sauce off his face, out of his eyes and hair and off the ceiling from which new lumps are constantly plummeting down.

At this point the pasta water, this time with the pasta in it, boils over again.

Male friends by now prostrate.

Me in rage.

Female friends (how could such angels in human form have MARRIED these schmucks?) glide to rescue, restore kitchen, make pasta sauce (just one) by conventional means, clear up debris, stack dishwasher, set it going and only giggle occasionally.

The only grain of comfort left to cling to is that the wife has slept through all this, she's in Manchester tomorrow, and by the time she gets back the whole shame-inducing nightmare will have been forgotten, won't it? 'Course it will.

And anyway, if someone does tell her I'll say they're exaggerating, and the red lump-shaped blotches all over my face will have gone, surely?

As I climb into bed it seems to be rocking more than can be accounted for by the booze.

Then there's a snort, a guffaw and a snigger all at once, and a small voice says, 'Hey, Blotchy, tell us about planning, then!'

'In Saudi Arabia,' I tell her, 'I need only say "I divorce you" three times and you'd be history.'

'Aah,' she snortles, 'but in Saudi Arabia not even Keith Floyd can get a drink.'

I don't see the connection myself.

Cookery is only about showing off for those people who can delegate the daily grind. Ask those three-star Michelin boys how many potatoes they peel these days. Once you're into the family-nutrition guilt trap, cookery is all about camouflaging something that's good for them as something else that tastes nice. To all children these two options are mutually exclusive. Any food scientist who can come up with a freshly picked, lightly steamed green vegetable that looks and tastes exactly like a chip with a few Heinz baked beans adhering to it will be a millionaire overnight.

My number-three son is an ardent fan of that literary giant, Sam Watterson, creator of Calvin and Hobbes, the funniest cartoon strip ever invented. (I went into our local Waterstone's to get one of the annuals last Christmas. 'Do you have things like Calvin and Hobbes or Asterix annuals?' said I.

'We do, sir, which do you want?'

'What difference does it make?'

'Aaah, you see, you'll find Asterix in the children's section!')

Joe's favourite Calvinism is the one where Calvin is sitting at the dinner table after his mum has served up, and he asks for a clean plate.

He does this on the grounds that someone has barfed on his.

Vegetarian cookery, more than anything else, lends itself to this reaction. The progression goes like this: hot-stuff cook (me) gets to be Houseworm and takes on nutritional responsibility for veggie wife and veggie children.

Non-veggie son and self easy . . . chuck us a chop and we're happy. No need to plan twenty-four hours in advance and soak pebble-like lentils (some of which invariably turn out to BE pebbles) in water until they're soft enough to cook sufficiently to form the basic ingredient and nutritional mainstay of some Kurdish casserole with a hurricane-force fart-factor. So what happens is this:

Monday: Baked Potatoes with Cheese in and Salad (there go spuds and cheese as main course)

Tuesday: Spaghetti with Pesto and Tomato Salad (there goes pasta)

Wednesday: Quiche and Green Beans and sauté potatoes (there goes eggs)

Thursday: Glamorgan Sausages, Mash and Peas (there goes fritters – and here comes cheese again)

Friday: Cheese-and-Onion Pasties and something or other (and that's cheese by three)

Saturday: Er . . .

    'Come on, come on, you haven't even done a week yet.'

    OK, Veggie Curry and Rice with Poppadams?

    'a) It's slosh with lumps in and b) the children won't eat it.'

    . . . So we'll give 'em pasta. Macaroni Cheese.

    'You're repeating yourself.'

    OK, how about butter-bean pie? . . . er . . .

See, already, only six days down the line, you're into some sloshy item with lumps in, tomato-and-onion-based, that may taste OK but not even putting a cheesy pastry crust on it can conceal its predigested nature. It's the fibrous quality of meat or fish that vegetables and pulses lack, and anyone who tells you that tofu is a perfect substitute has neither cooked nor eaten it. Where were we? Aah, yes:

Sunday: Sweetcorn Fritters, Roast Potatoes (it should be mash, but we've had that once) and some blasted greenery or other that isn't peas or beans. How about courgettes, for example?

And there you (or rather I) go. Only one meal a day for seven days and the vegetable (in more ways than one) imagination has run headlong into the buffers.

I'm repeating fried things and pasta already.

It's all very well for Madhur Jaffrey to produce mouth-watering recipes involving Dhal, Aloo Bokhara, Amazu Shoga and Asakusa Nori (all of which succeed in making vegetarian dishes sound the way they look), but being veggie doesn't make the average five-year-old any less conservative.

'Yuk' is kidspeak for 'I say, old man, we're not having any of that ghastly foreign muck, are we? For God's sake take it away and bring me a decent treacle sponge.'

You try it.

Produce just seven vegetarian meals without shoving in eggs, cheese, fritters, pasta or slosh with lumps in it more than once. And then see how many of your efforts your children will actually EAT! God alone knows what vegan children get. Macrobiotic tie-dyed rice, I shouldn't wonder.

It's not true that they don't grow out of it, but it takes years and travel (preferably leavened with a good dose of deprivation) to broaden the culinary mind. Sons numbers one through two are OK, I guess, but Joe and Rosie are still a nutritionist's nightmare.

The number-one son was cured of all his gastronomic pernicketyness by the simple expedient of sending him to Russia for three weeks to stay with a family in Moscow. He describes such meat as he got as 'mystery meat' in that its spongy texture resembled no part of any animal from quail to horse that he had previously happily consumed, and he gagged on the gristly bits.

Home cooking is now something he takes pains to be grateful for.

Number Two, being the first vegetarian, was cured by the equally simple expedient of sending him to an extremely expensive boarding-school whose catering department's culinary imagination really does make me look like Raymond Blanc on speed.

Joe is different. When tired, just the sight of something he has never seen before and which I have spent two hours preparing can reduce him to floods of tears, rage and resentment.

'Why do you always keep giving me NEW things?' he'll scream. 'I hate them . . . and I hate YOU! Mummy gives me things I LIKE!' (The way to a father's heart, this.)

'LIKE WHAT?' I yell back.

'LIKE ALPEN!'

Alpen? As in muesli? As in breakfast? As in 'perhaps if we put yoghurt on it it would balance out the politically incorrect sugar level'? Yup. That's the stuff. Alpen is to Joe what Chocolate-Frosted Sugar Bombs are to his friend Calvin.

It not only keeps him going, but probably accounts for the hyperactivity as well. A bowlful, and I mean FULL, at breakfast is reinforced by another one as soon as he gets in the door from school (this one he shares with his cockatiel, which stands IN the bowl while Joe watches telly and spoons up muesli from between its legs). From this, he gains sufficient strength to resist all pleas to do his homework until, weakened and exhausted by the antipodean antics of the televisually challenged on *Neighbours*, he collapses in a heap at the sight of some culinary masterpiece lovingly prepared by his father, and the only thing that will right the wrong, renew his morale and fortify him for even a token attack on his homework is (aah, you guessed) another bowl of Alpen.

He is the only child on earth (surely?) who eats Alpen sandwiches. Not only Alpen, but Alpen-and-yoghurt sandwiches. Not long ago he was offered a peach by his grandfather.

'Can I put Alpen on it?'

Rosie is different. No less difficult, just different. With her it's pasta. She will eat other things, occasionally, but definitely not for breakfast. Breakfast is reheated pasta with grated cheese onna top, and listen, buddy; that pasta had better be the right SHAPE, see? She'll eat any sort of pasta, but she has to decide which, when and with what. For example, cheese sauce is designed to go on penne, or possibly macaroni, while tomato sauce can only be served on spaghetti and then only once she's been asked.

If she arrives to find the deed done, you're in the pooh, as she so elegantly expresses it. Pesto can be served on anything except shells, and that's my decision, not hers; made on the grounds that if you allow people to eat pasta shells full of anything as delicious as pesto, the next thing you know they'll be scooping it out of the jar with a spoon.

So, given all that, what does the wise little Houseworm DO about catering? I shall tell you, because you're nice. The wise Houseworm cooks as little or as much, as originally or as traditionally, as *haute* or as *bas* as he pleases, subject to the following rules:

1) Never run out of bread, cheese or Alpen

2) Never cook less than 2 kilos of pasta a week

3) Keep the fruit bowl full

This personal nutritional theory sprang fully formed from an American (I think) experiment in which children were allowed to eat whatever they liked from a range of food-stuffs from Toblerone to macrobiotic rice via sashimi and pepperoni pizza, and within forty-eight hours, having started out bingeing on sweeties, the kids were all consuming a perfectly balanced diet.

Mostly, I hope, the children will eat something their metabolism requires before rickets sets in, and if they don't then all I can say is that it serves them right. The other thing the Houseworm should keep in the forefront of what gets laughingly referred to as his mind, is that he must on no account fall into the trap of asking the little sods what they want to eat.

I did this for a while with the result that Rosie thinks she lives in a sort of short-order heaven, where the chef will simply rustle up whatever item she selects from the menu she carries in her head.

On a day when I have decided to broaden her mind by introducing her to a (very mild) Thai Curry, she doesn't even look at it before she informs me that what she wants for supper is a coddled egg with pasta in it.

Children, even ours, have friends.

Said friends are frequently the happy possessors of parents, either or both of whom may be responsible for the revolting tastes, manners and eating habits of their children, but neither of whom is around when their unspeakable brat says, 'Yuk! Wotsis'en? Don't you got no chips 'n' ketchup?'

'It's Boston Baked Beans,' you say. 'It's very nice.'

'No it's not! Baked beans come in tins.'

(Pause here, if you will, for a small culinary anecdote: Jane Grigson, doyenne of food writers, was complaining to a friend that she didn't know what to give the children for supper. Friend suggested baked beans. 'Darling, what a wonderful idea, but it would take so long!')

'What,' you enquire of Attila the brat through clenched teeth, 'do you eat at home?'

'Chips 'n' ketchup 'n' PROPER baked beans.'

'Anything else?'

'Nah. Sometimes Chicken McNuggets.'

Go with the flow, best beloved.

Always keep a tin of Heinz Beans (NOT the reduced sugar kind . . . no-one wants to improve this kid's health) in the larder; a bag of Oven Chips in the freezer and a squeezy bottle of ketchup in the fridge. Even your immaculately behaved and scrupulously polite offspring might occasionally feel the need for a little gastronomic slumming, and if this sort of diet isn't good for them, GOOD!

CHAPTER TWELVE

Health and Efficiency

'What do you want, clean or tidy? I don't do both.'

ME

TOWARDS THE MIDDLE OF THE MAJOR YEAR, I HAD HAD time to identify my strengths, such as they were, and at least some of my weaknesses. I spotted some of the latter even without the help of the Househead, who by the beginning of June was working fourteen-hour days at home when she wasn't working eighteen-hour days elsewhere. She therefore had less and less time available for dispensing instruction and enlightenment, and I had time to brood; especially on such matters as domestic hygiene.

Ever since 1974, when a Health Visitor was despatched by the DHSS to check up on how the wife and I were coping with our brand-new first-born, I have been profoundly sceptical of both the intentions and the effectiveness of those set in local authority over us. She arrived, this educator and guardian of the defenceless child against the ignorance and viciousness of its natural parents, with a Players No. 6 glued into the corner of her mouth, and around this she produced the sort of cough that makes tuberculosis sound like a case of athlete's foot.

She interrupted Penny mid-feed and took our baby onto her lap. He, deprived of titty, proceeded to root blindly about at which point the official said, 'Aaaah, look, he's yawning!' Even I knew better than that. She then rang a bell and when he turned his head she declared that there was nothing wrong with his hearing and left. This and other personal experiences have led me to believe that the last person to be given a say in how we live our lives should be anyone who applied for the job, whether or not they have attended the three-day training-course.

The last remaining bastion of the freedom to give yourself food poisoning is the home, because not even Edwina Currie would try sending the Environmental Health Police into the Englishman's castle to monitor the temperature of his fridge and the date stamp on his cod fish fingers. It is our duty to revel in this freedom, and extend its bounds at every opportunity. The committed Houseworm will only patronize those shops who keep, for the benefit of the connoisseur, unpasteurized milk straight from the local farm, ditto cheeses, with eggs that are from Mrs Jones' flock that has never been salmonella tested and if she has anything to do with it never will be. Only by doing this is the Houseworm likely to protect his family from the 39 per cent increase in salmonella poisoning that immediately followed Mrs Currie's slaughter of 3.3 million chickens to protect the public.

The local shopkeeper will need to know you, since these items are not generally on public view and their purchase involves a great deal more nudging and winking than the acquisition of a copy of *Men Only* off the top shelf, or the surreptitious purchase of 'something for the weekend'. And if your five-year-old *does* get the trots, so what? All the more immunity and resistance will be built up for the next time. Furthermore, the items thus acquired will add to your life's pleasures by the simple expedient of tasting of something (even, possibly, of themselves), unlike the pasteurized, heat-treated, ultrasonically sterilized products so highly recommended for our nutrition by the Bumleys and Gummers set in authority over us.

Consider, if you will, two strapping nineteen-year-old lads taking a gap-year trip for five months travelling overland from Hong Kong to Western Europe via Tibet, India and Nepal. Let's say one of 'em comes from a normal home. Clean, conscientious, houseproud and hygienic, he has been brought up to be a pillar of *mens sana in corpore* and all that.

T'other belongs to us, and has been brought up in this Houseworm's idea of healthy living.

The breakfast bread gets sliced on a breadboard from which the cat's backside has been removed but one millisecond since.

The butter, which I got out (to soften it) when I made the early tea, by breakfast displays those decorative striations that only a cat's tongue can impart, and where we mostly drop the toast between toaster and table is on the dog.

Guess which youf got amoebic dysentery and had to be nursed back to health by which, only to be carted off to hospital in Delhi with a temperature of 105. Uhuh! That's the one.

In this Houseworm's family the bugs on our insides are a match for all invasive strains of beastie, not excluding cholera or the Black Death. Comes from living where the Houseworm hasn't got time for all that 'round the bend' stuff and doesn't see the Harpic and Jeyes ads admonishing him to 'safeguard his family' by 'killing all known germs . . . DEAD'. The reason for this is that even if the television is switched on, he has long since switched off.

The Houseworm's guidelines to domestic hygiene, health, safety and hazardous waste are as follows:

FRIDGE

If in doubt, stick it in the fridge. Someone (something?) may eat it.

If it's already in the fridge and it's got grey fur on it, it's probably a cat clearing up after lunch.

If it's still there a week or so later and the fur has changed colour from grey to green, chuck it out (even if it IS the cat).

If you've just made it, and your children have indicated that it scores 99.9 on the Yuk scale, put it in the fridge. After two weeks you'll be glad to throw it out. If it's fizzy and it's pink it's probably taramasalata that's well past its 'use by' date. It's probably past its 'give it to the cat by' date as well.

Nothing is ever past its 'give it to the dog by' date.

LARDER

The larder is where you put things that are still too warm to put in the fridge. You then forget about them with the result that in a week (or even less in warm weather) you can chuck them straight out without having to go through the ritual of cluttering up the fridge.

If you leave the larder door open you can reduce your involvement to picking up the broken bits of whatever it was in, that the dog leaves on the floor.

FREEZER

This is where you store whatever it is that is so delicious you want to make compost out of it in 1996. Whatever it was when it went into the freezer, within a year the label will have fallen off, the wrapping will have biodegraded, the colour will have deteriorated to a uniform dull grey with freezer-burn streaks of pale brown, and you will be past caring.

The only reason you're digging it out now and throwing it away is that you need to make room for some of this year's crop of early carrots the gardening Houseworm (you) gets so excited about, or, later on, for runner beans, which as usual are so plentiful that if you see another one before Christmas you'll heave.

By Christmas the freezer will have worked its magic and you'll have forgotten all about runner beans for another year. (See chapter on gardening provisionally entitled: 'Why, in God's Name?')

On the compost heap of the future it will thaw into a grey pile that makes you think your wife has been freezing something the dog brought up, and in thirty seconds the dog will be bringing it up again.

LAVATORIES

While it is true to say that whoever uses the lavatory generally feels a lot better for it than the person who uses it next, the Houseworm will not yield to the temptation to display 'Forest Glade'-type air fresheners.

These simply replace a nasty smell by a nastier one, and the nastier one isn't even naturally disgusting. Somebody went into a laboratory and thought it up.

Death does not 'lurk in the U-bend', asphyxiation by ammonia lurks in the carpet all round the bowl.

This is the recipient of the directional shortcomings of all drunks, male children under twenty-one and ladies in more of a hurry than is good for them (or the carpet). There is no cure for this hygiene black spot other than to tile all lavatories and steam clean with pure bleach or aqua regia or both, once every twenty-four hours.

Pure bleach, descaler and other products can be emptied into the bowl in the hopes of reducing staining below the waterline without recourse to industrial Marigolds and wire wool; but pure concentrated bleach, applied via splash-back to the fundament of the five-year-old, can lead to the Houseworm missing a whole episode of *Lovejoy*.

BATHROOMS

Nobody ever died of ring poisoning, except possibly Wagner, so the wise Houseworm leaves the one round the bath alone.

If you must, I guess you can follow Shirley Conran's advice and put a capful of some detergent like washing-up liquid in the bath every time you run it, but your children might get eczema and you'll all end up smelling of laboratory lemon rind.

Injuries of industrial proportions can be inflicted by getting into a bath that's had some skin-softening gunk emptied into it. It is better to forbid the gunk than go through the graft of getting it off, even if you survive the fall.

In all multi-bath households (those where lots of people want one, rather than those with lots of baths), the 'run a clean bath only when you can no longer see the bottom' rule is one that both saves water and builds community spirit.

It's dangerous to feud with someone who's going to get this evening's bath ahead of you. Mind you, he'll only tell you what he did after you get in.

CEILINGS, WALLS AND FLOORS

Cobwebs are not only harmless, they can be both fascinating and instructive, and reduce the bluebottle population.

Furthermore, should you have failed, yet again, to buy elastoplast, they are reputed to be good for staunching bleeding.

Active crane-fly and spider populations ought to be encouraged as they amuse cats and children and are environmentally and ecologically PC.

Walls pose no hazard to health, not even if they remain unwashed. Washing them, after all, may very well remove the toothpaste, felt-tip and blood fresco the number-three son and overnight guest created on the wall in the spare room.

Who are we, mere Houseworms, to deprive unborn generations of the juvenilia of a future Warhol or Pollock?

Dust balls, especially in houses with oak-strip floors and a high pet population, tend to grow within days into a sort of ethereal tumbleweed, rolling through the hall on the faintest draught as down Main Street, Deadman's Gulch, in a Nor' Easter.

They are liable to need removing every now and then.

The way to do this is not with a mop or broom which simply move them about and make you sneeze, but with a vacuum cleaner.

This means you can vacuum both wooden floors and carpeted areas at the same time, and avoid like the plague any suggestion that wooden floors should be polished. Polished floors are highly dangerous and no doubt the subject of some directive or other; and even if you get 'em nicely buffed up without some damn fool breaking their neck in the pools of Traffic wax, the animals will trail slobber, wet paws or bleeding rodents across them in no time.

Leave it.

As Quentin Crisp pointed out: 'After the first four years it doesn't get any dirtier.'

I consider that my attitude to health, hygiene and immunity from both diseases and council interference is a fair and just one, but that is not to say that there are not those who sometimes wish it LOOKED as if I cared about appearances.

But I do, madam, I do.

I may not do 'clean', but I do do 'tidy'. Tidy is for people who have no desire to pick things up other than to put other things under them. Do not pick things up with cleaning in mind.

If you pick up or move a microwave, for example, you might very well find beneath it such things as nightmares are made of and that even you might baulk at simply covering up again.

The solution is obvious. Do NOT, under any circumstances, lift or move anything beneath or behind which may lurk items or substances about which you do not wish to know. These objects include cookers, fridges, freezers, washing-machines, dishwashers and all other appliances whose very nature seems to declare *'Nemo me impune movet'*.

Some of these items are such that while you cannot see behind or beneath them, small desperate furry creatures can take refuge there; and there, because the cats take turns guarding their escape route, they die of their injuries or starvation. Nature being what it is, there shortly emanates from beneath whatever it is a smell that makes following UT into the downstairs lavatory a positive treat by comparison, but bear with it.

On no account investigate, for you will find not only the cause of the present sussuration, blown into abhorring, but his predeceased uncles, aunts and Cousin Esmeralda, whose corpse is now the consistency of very old, dried toffee and as easy to remove, so DON'T DO IT!

All these appliances have their place, usually tailor-made little or large niches out of which it is a perfect bugger to get them, and into which they are invariably impossible to replace without tearing both the flooring and the skin off your knuckles.

LAUNDRY

There was once, long ago, an advertising campaign for some detergent or other which made a great deal of what it called 'THE UNDERSTAINS'. I shall pause, here, while you vomit. Better? Good.

Now there are some exceptional items, which, be they ever so tidy, need to be clean as well. Among them the Houseworm will find dirty socks (esp. those of adolescent males, for some reason), dirty underpants (anybody's) and handkerchiefs belonging to those people sporting a particularly heavy head cold. So these all have to be washed, and while they're in the machine you might as well get a few understains out of the armpits of shirts and tomato ketchup out of the front of Joe's jumper. Boiling (handkerchiefs) or handwashing (anything) may look good on *Upstairs, Downstairs*, but the 1990s require, and so do I, that things can be washed and dried by machine.

Because there ISN'T an ironing machine, I don't do any. (The title's a JOKE, for God's sake!)

Anything that claims, by means of hieroglyphics on the label, that it cannot be machine-washed and tumble-dried should immediately be subjected to these experiences, preferably at very high temperatures. After this, the garment's owner will no longer want it and it can be safely jettisoned.

A very long time ago, when we were young and the sexual revolution was rolling happily along in the mid to late sixties, we (the about-to-be wife and I) did a little university matchmaking at our flat in a small Scottish fishing village. Before our dinner guests arrived we carefully made up a double bed on the floor, out of mattresses, old track suits, our only clean pair of white sheets, and assorted blankets, ex-army overcoats and damask curtains.

Scottish fishing villages are still cold, but now the flats are centrally heated. THEN, let me tell you, the temperature inside was only greater than that outside by the difference in the wind-chill factor.

All went well (the couple are still married and extremely famous) and the following morning, after they set off for one of those long romantic wind-swept walks on the West Sands so beloved of St Andrews University undergraduates and the makers of *Chariots of Fire*, we went in to make the bed. I think our mistake was in using a pair of red, non-colour-fast track suit bottoms as an underblanket between white sheets. It is not a mistake I will repeat, nor the loving couple live down.

In normal circumstances, however, especially once the heyday in the blood is cold (any time after 6 p.m. in my case), beds have the great advantage that in making them the sheets get covered up.

Throw-rugs and scatter cushions can be made to serve a similarly covert purpose.

Covering up unsightly and probably unhygienic marks on anything is a far better option than scouring the works of Ms Conran for some Victorian hints on removing bubble-gum stains from Axminster. (What I would like Ms Conran to do is update her seminal work to tell this Houseworm how to peel old panty-liners, with or without 'wings', off the bin liner so that I don't tear it – the bin liner – and can use it again and earn an ecological Brownie point. But that's by the by.)

We are talking TIDY, right? So 'what the eye don't see . . .'

Let that be the Houseworm's watchword: discretion is the better part of velour, especially if someone's been sick on it.

CHAPTER THIRTEEN

Usage and Abusage

'It is only too easy to compel a sensitive human being to feel guilty about anything.'

M.I. SEIDEN

'DADDY, I'VE GOT A ITCHY PAGINA,' IS A PLEA GUARAN-teed to strike fear into the heart of any father, but in the case of the Houseworm, responsible as he is for the physical, pastoral and spiritual well-being of his offspring male and female, the complaint sends icy trickles of apprehension crawling up his spine. Pausing only to whisper a brief prayer to Santa Marietta della Infanta, I say: 'It's "vagina", not "pagina", and how long has it been itching?'

'All daaaayyy, Daddeeeee. Loook!'

I defy any reader, male or female, to assert that if they came upon a middle-aged gent closly examining, or worse still applying ointment to, the crotch of a five-year-old girl, their initial assumption would be that here was a concerned father dealing with a minor infection in one of his children.

Mmmh?

Oh no you wouldn't! I have been there and I know.

Thanks to the machinations of the more lunatic fringes of the feminist movement (all men are rapists, child-abusers and probably readers of the *Daily Telegraph* to boot) and the dubious anal-dilatation enthusiasms of Marietta of blessed memory, a minor genito-urinary infection can get the Houseworm a lot of sidelong glances from the local medical establishment.

I took her to our GP.

(This is a lie. I got her mother to take her to our GP.)

She got a locum who, having established that Rosie's father was a Houseworm, said: 'Vaginal infection? That's VERY unusual,' and he gave the wife an extremely side-long glance.

It isn't *very* unusual. It's not even *quite* unusual; it's extremely common, as anyone with a working knowledge of where small children stick their fingers would know. As HE would have known had he not been got at by the combined forces of the 'All Dads are Abusers' department of the Social Services, and the tabloid editors, for whom 'Dad Abuses Home Alone Daughter' means 50,000 more papers sold.

I kept my mouth shut and trusted in Doctor–Patient confidentiality and Penelope Leach (*Baby and Child*, since you ask, pages 382 & 496). Nevertheless, I have this recurring nightmare: it all starts with Dr Very Unusual sending in the Social Services, and culminates in the arrival on our doorstep of the Thought Police who have come to talk to Rosie.

Our daughter, who is delighted to entertain any audience and has so far informed two plumbers and the man who came to read the gas meter that her 'daddy and mummy sometimes want to hug each other in the mornings but she won't let them because it's time to make the tea and sometimes they say it's still dark but she makes them get up and put their clothes on anyway', is in her element, and the interrogation goes like this:

TP: Hullo, Rosie. Where do you sleep?

Rosie: In Mummy and Daddy's bed.

TP: Really? Why don't you sleep in your own bed?

Rosie: Because it's nicer in the big bed.

TP: I see. And does your mummy ever go away?

Rosie: Yes, every week.

TP: And where do you sleep then?

Rosie: In my daddy's bed with him.

TP: Mm. Tell me, Rosie, what sort of pyjamas do you wear?

Rosie: Sometimes I wear a T-shirt or a nightie but mostly I take them off.

TP: Why, Rosie?

Rosie: 'Cos I don't like them.

TP: What sort of pyjamas does your daddy wear?

Rosie: He doesn't wear any.

TP: I see. So when your mummy is away your daddy has you sleeping in his bed and neither of you are wearing pyjamas?

Rosie: And in the morning we have wrestling matches 'cos he doesn't want to get up and make the tea.

TP: All right, Rosie. Now I want you to get your favourite teddy bear because we're taking you to where you'll be safe.

Me: WHAT?!

TP: I'd advise you to say nothing, sir. The Social Services will look after her, and if there's nothing in what she says I'm sure you'll get her back in no time. In the mean time, we will be asking a court to refuse parental access and your wife will be hearing from us about her collusion.

You think this is paranoid? If it is, in the time-honoured phrase, it doesn't mean the bastards aren't out to get you.

Throughout all this paranoia, I hear distant voices crooning something that sounds like 'The lady doth protest too much, methinks', so I call a psychologist pal for reassurance.

'Forget it,' says he. 'I hate pyjamas, but I've been wearing them ever since our daughter took to getting into bed with us.' This, I have to keep reminding myself, is a guy whose job it is to know how people think.

Any minute now, I think to myself, we're all going to be back in the looking-glass world of the Dutch Reformed Church, rumoured to have condemned sexual intercourse between married couples in a standing position on the grounds that while it isn't intrinsically sinful, it could lead to dancing.

We are a tactile family, and proud of it, too. One of my formative memories of 'how real men behave' was watching with Anglo-Saxon astonishment as an Afrikaans friend, aged all of seventeen, kissed his father with unselfconscious affection ON THE LIPS! My astonishment was not unmixed with admiration, and I still get a glow of pleasure when all our sons dish out kisses and hugs to their parents with complete impartiality, but there is still enough good old British Public School Stiff Upper Lip Garbage in me to wonder what my male friends might think if they saw this sort of thing going on. I don't exactly MIND, you see, but it is interesting.

In the isolated world of the Houseworm, where contact with the real world is made through newspapers and radio (because you can't sort the laundry and watch television, that's why), it is easy to begin to think that maybe there is something a BIT funny about yourself after all. I ask a mum if her five-year-old would like to come and play with Rosie, and I'm SURE she's thinking about who's going to take her blue-eyed darling to the lavatory and will my wife be there or am I going to be in sole charge, and what sort of bloke am I anyway?

What she's actually thinking, of course, is, Thank God . . . now I can have the afternoon to myself, but I don't know that.

It is while these two little girls are spending the afternoon together, mostly in the privacy of Rosie's bedroom, where they shriek, giggle and for some deeply mysterious reason find it necessary to remove all their clothes before making a secret camp out of the bedclothes, the bookshelf and the top bunk, that I gain a small insight into where my guilt trip originates. If I come up stairs the screams of hysteria reach migraine level as they yell 'DON'T COME IN' at the tops of their voices. As if I'd dare. I remember some totally awful American comedian whose act consisted entirely of enticing young children to talk frankly about their parents in front of the sort of live audience who find a lisped 'My mummy's got big blue knickers' amusing to the point of apoplexy. What they would have made of Rosie's eager disclosures defies belief.

Pausing only to think what her friend's parents would make of their daughter's supper-time description of how 'she and Rosie took all their clothes off and then Rosie's daddy gave them chocolate biscuits', I took Radio 4 up to the attic, where I had earlier identified a rich area for housewormery.

This was going to involve getting eleven years' worth of what the Househead had stuffed into the attic in unlabelled bin-liners 'just in case', down the steps, then the stairs, then out into the yard, into the car and down to the tip for recycling without any member of the family becoming aware of what I was up to. Had Rosie had no friend to distract her, every item in every bag would immediately have become yet another thing that she couldn't live without, regardless of the fact that she's lived perfectly well without it for the past five years. She gets it from her mother.

So there I am, *Woman's Hour* burbling merrily away in the background, trying to extract heavy black bin-liners from the corner of the attic behind the empty cardboard boxes awaiting some possible future need to pack up the Hi-Fi or the computer, both of which, I realize, we sold at a car-boot sale three years ago.

(The *Woman's Hour* programme that originally got me hooked, so that I now make up part of the male 30 per cent of their listeners, contained an interview with a quiltmaker who has a shop in our home town. Fascinating, I thought.

'Now this was traditionally women's work, was it not?' Jenni Murray asked her. 'The work was communal and a lot of women's themes would have been addressed, wouldn't they?'

The local lady misheard the word and floundered.

'Seams? Well yes, they did make seams . . . er . . .'

You could *hear* her thinking, WOMEN's seams? Wot's she on?

This made me laugh so much I seldom miss an opportunity of letting Jenni Murray brighten up my day.)

I am just exerting enough pull on a bag to allow me to extract it (or alternatively tear it, spilling its contents over a wide area whilst I simultaneously step back, miss the floored bit and put my foot between the joists and through the bathroom ceiling) when I hear Ms Murray's voice announcing that the subject for today's debate and phone in is to be 'Should Men Be Allowed to Look After Children?'. So astonished am I at the possibilities conjured up by this that I let go of the bag (without tearing it), step back in amazement and put my foot between the joists and through the bathroom ceiling.

I remain, held fast by my lath-and-plaster ankle-cuff, and listen to some quite serious people asserting that in the light of a recent Tyneside case of assault by a male carer, the Government should institute in nursery schools a 'Gender Appropriate Policy' which would ensure that no forty-year-old father of three could take a toddler to the lavatory unless accompanied by a female human. Any female human, in fact.

I gently extract my foot and go quietly back to work, so as not to miss anything. Us Houseworms have to know how to keep our noses clean, after all. First we heard that paedophiles queue up for childcare jobs 'like alcoholics trying to get work in a bar'. Next up was some poor guy, with qualifications as a childminder coming out of his ears, who'd had to go to America to get work. No agency here would touch him. He didn't get a lot of sympathy.

What about me? I am thinking. Most abuse happens in

the home, and the abuser is nearly always a member of the family, right? Surely there was going to be some suggestion that I ought to be stopped? After all, 10 feet below me, two five-year-olds with no clothes on are constantly yelling at me not to come in, or else requesting bribes in the form of chocolate Hob-Nobs. This could be my salvation. Please, Ms Murray, turn me in. GET ME OUTTA HERE!

The downside about this way of getting out of the childcare is that it's only a matter of time before the extremely on-the-ball producers of *Woman's Hour* recommend, in the light of the Beverley Allitt case, a 'Gender Appropriate Policy' for paediatric units, and all the nurses will have to be men or at least be supervised by men. Also, of course, the incidence of babies being snatched from prams by disturbd women will lead to a men-only policy in the high street, so it'll be back to the shopping for yours truly.

Me, I go back to the bin-liners. After I've dropped five bags full of clothes down the loft-ladder and replaced the empty boxes 'just in case', I hear louder than ever giggles and stick my head through the hatch over the landing. All my carefully tied bin-bags are open, their contents spread widely about the landing, and Rosie and her friend are now wearing a couple of curtains and a cricket pad each and are shouting, 'Can we keep them, Can we keep them?' at the top of their lungs. Time, I decide, for tea.

I manage, by dint of further offerings of chocolate biscuits, to impress upon the two of them that tea will only be served to those wearing a full complement of regulation clothes among which a minimum of one pair of knickers (each) will be obligatory, and further, that refreshments will only be served in the kitchen. Since the visitor is being collected in an hour, I wish her to witness the presence of the Prime Ministerial biographer who is due down from her eyrie for her tea, and to have time to forget, before she goes home, that she and her hostess spent most of the afternoon stark naked under a sheet in a bedroom screaming at her friend's daddy not to come in.

CHAPTER FOURTEEN

Fun and Games

'Serious sport has nothing to do with fair play. It is bound up with hatred, jealousy, boastfulness, disregard of all rules and sadistic pleasure in witnessing violence: in other words it is war minus the shooting.'

GEORGE ORWELL

THROUGHOUT THE YEAR MY DOMESTIC PREDICAMENT engendered in my Houseworm's heaving heart the desire to get out of the house at least once a week to indulge in some activity more strenuous than bringing in the logs, and with more social give and take than helping Joe with his homework. My excuse for this desire is the usual one about being stuck in the house/car/supermarket all day and only having dwarves to talk to. BUT:

Question: What is the difference between a working man and a working woman?

Answer: After work a woman gets on with something useful; a man plays sport.

The transition from human to Houseworm has not as yet completely excised from my psyche the desire to escape from domestic bliss into squash, tennis, gliding, ANYTHING, even to the point of playing damn-fool games with Macho Mike (q.v.). Female guardians of the hearth do not, apart from the occasional aerobics class, do this. Why not?

Or if they do, the odd tennis morning is more by way of being a social event than a battle to the death. But men don't just want to get out of the house; after all, they've BEEN out of the house all day, and as for socializing, what are office banter, business lunches and post-work brownies all about? No, what they want is to kill something or someone so they can drag their triumph home to impress the wife.

Remember the rock hyrax?

Sometimes it's hobbies. These can be a lot worse. Take Colin: wife, two children and a passion for car-boot sales. The trouble is, that if you're a golf widow, the old fart simply takes out his clubs, buzzes off for the day, and then comes back to replace his clubs, or at least get you to replace them for him, while he regales you with the fascinating anecdote of how he missed that twelve-foot, right-to-left putt at the fifteenth to lose the match to some snot-nosed whippersnapper with no golfing etiquette and lousy dress sense. (What he doesn't tell you is that dressed in plus-two knickerbockers in Prince of Wales check and knee-length tartan socks, he was so excited to be over the water and on the green in two that he lunged at the putt and actually putted it straight back into the lake. It was at this point that his opponent, dressed in jeans and an Iron Maiden T-shirt, laughed, and earned himself the old boy's undying hatred.)

But the car-boot widow has a different problem to contend with.

She waves him off on a Saturday morning, complete with train-spotter's Thermos and woolly hat, and by the time he gets back he's got a set of ashtrays showing scenes of Majorca, two 1950s magazine racks complete with issues of *National Geographic*, 1964–68, and a mowing machine that, were it thirty years older, might be of interest to the local museum of mechanics, or were it thirty years younger, might work.

Colin sets off each weekend for any and every sale within 30 miles. His hunting cry of, 'Hey, that's good value,' does not mean that the item under discussion has any relevance to his own circumstances, that it might actually be useful or indeed be of such a size or shape that his by now non-existent storage space may somehow accommodate it.

No, he wants it because he found it and it's cheap, and despite his protests that 'it might come in useful, you never know', he is going to require his wife to find space for it somewhere in their quite small house and in the future to dust it, pull it out, clean behind it and replace it for ever and ever, weekly.

Colin just seems to think that a passion for car-boot sales MUST take priority over anything else; children, Sunday lunch, laundry and sexual intercourse included. (OK, that last is a guess, but you get the idea.)

Now these blokes, along with their opposite numbers in the fields of gambling, polo, golf, cricket, hockey, birdwatching, huntin' shootin' an' fishin' and train-spotting are all getting out of the house out of which they have got every working day (don't want ter be under t' wife's feet all day, do yer lad?), and leaving their housekeeper/ laundryperson/cook/valet/sex object/nanny/wet nurse and childminder in the house, in which she has been all day every day except for shopping, to get on with what they doggedly and wittily continue to describe as 'doing nothing all day'.

I mean they really believe this, and like the White Queen they are capable of believing at least six impossible things before breakfast, including that while their darling helpmeets are doing nothing all day, they are perfectly capable of acquiring several departmental responsibilities none the less. Go on, ask one of them. Say: 'Where's your daughter keep her sweatshirts?' This will not only get you a very old-fashioned look if you're a male friend, but the following reply: 'Not my department, ol' boy. Have a beer.'

Try it with any department covered by the list of responsibilities outlined above and the reply will be the same. I'm beginning to think that the only reason he knows where the beer's kept is that she might be out doing nothing at the shops when he wants one.

It is these same professional men whose idea of a good time is dictated partly by their desire not to be part of the domestic round (understandable) and partly by the desire to get back to nature and find their spiritual dimension by roping themselves to six other guys and getting soaking wet, totally knackered and cold to the point of hypothermia before being hauled off a particularly scenic bit of Helvellyn by the mountain rescue boys (incomprehensible).

OK, so I'm not exactly last in the queue for a bit of recreation but my escape from the Houseworm's lot involves gliding, an activity which, given British weather, involves a great deal more socializing than flying and where you have a sporting chance of encountering a woman; even, God forbid, a woman instructor.

Not, more than once, is this so with PAINTBALL.

Robert Bly would LOVE those guys. Paintball, or Wargames or call it what you will, is an activity (sport? game? personal development therapy?) involving groups of people, mainly men, pretending to be Rambo, running around woodland sites in combat fatigues and 'killing' each other using guns that fire exploding balls filled with paint. If you're hit, you're 'dead', but after five minutes in the 'dead' zone you can start again. Now the day I played there were several women among the players, all of whom had signed forms agreeing that they understood the game was dangerous, that they could get hurt and that they wouldn't sue the company that ran it if they were injured.

As it happened, the first victim that fell to my astonishingly (to me especially) accurate shooting was an 'enemy' soldier hiding behind a tree about 30 yards away. My single shot hummed across the clearing and slapped loudly against the hand holding the gun and burst white paint all over it. This exemplary shot was greeted by a very high-pitched cry of 'OW! Bloody hell. That HURT!' and the lady was ordered to the dead zone by a marshal who clearly thought women had no business being on a battlefield anyway.

I later found out that it did, in fact, hurt to get shot; and with a muzzle velocity of 300 feet per second, getting splatted on the forehead at a range of 15 feet could draw blood and raise a bump like an egg. I felt I should apologize, between games, for hurting this person, but I was accused of sexism. Balls, I would have apologized to a bloke as well, but it does seem daft to play a game which involves apologizing for winning.

The 'marshals', or organizers of this thing, are extremely serious about it and leap out from cover like Arnie Schwarzenegger, machine-gunning their gas carbines at such a rate that by the time you say, 'OW! OK I'm DEAD! Bloody hell, OW!' they've slammed another ten paintballs into your chest, head and hair.

This, for them, is no game. This is the Vietnam War rerun for their benefit. One of them told me he attended some martial arts class where a former SAS guy taught seven-year-olds (and, presumably, their twenty-year-old mental equivalents like him) how to drive someone's ribs through their lungs with a chair.

I don't know what sort of politics these sportsmen espouse, but I did notice that in South Africa the 'Training for War' programme of the AWB was a) devoid of women and b) particularly attractive to the sort of young men who go for all that 'male bonding' stuff.

What paintball made me realize was just how badly I did NOT want to do this for real, but it's different strokes for different folks, I guess, and anyway, I had to get back to get the children's supper.

Another example of the 'Me moron, you Jane' school of incomprehensible male activity is, *pace* Nick Hornby and his critically acclaimed *Fever Pitch*, the Wednesday-evening, Saturday-afternoon football match.

I'm not talking about playing, I'm talking about supporting a club and travelling miles only to see them lose, and HATING the other club's supporters and wanting to DIE if your lot get relegated, and arguing half of Monday morning at the office about some blind ref and the off-side-advantage rule.

I must confess, my bewilderment at this stuff is probably genetic. In the early Fifties my father used to take the pools coupons so thoughtfully thrust through his front door by eager young Littlewoods runners and carefully write 'I HOPE THEY ALL LOSE' across them.

He'd post them, too.

But I do have direct experience. For many years my favourite bank manager has been a devoted follower of West Ham, and every time he mentioned he was going to watch them play, I'd go through all the hilarious clichés about 'Got your flick-knife, then? Bog roll? Stomping boots? Tattoo?' and he would patiently, and sometimes impatiently, depending on how hilarious I thought I was being, explain that it wasn't like that, that he'd never seen any trouble, that he'd never hesitate to take his four-year-old along to a match, and that the strongest thing he drank was Bovril, and, finally, that if I wasn't such a prejudiced, blinkered, mindless clod he'd invite me to accompany him to a match.

I said no thanks I preferred myself the way I was.

Then one day he rang to say there was no way I could get out of it, he'd got his brother coming home on leave from the RAF in Cyprus, his oldest friend (and fellow West Ham supporter) coming back from the States and it was his birthday, and as a surprise he'd taken a box at QPR where West Ham were playing and I was to come and learn a thing or two. Lunch, he said, was included, as well as whatever I cared to drink except that during the match they lock up the booze cupboard.

This, thought I, I had to see.

Not knowing the form, I arrived early at the large Victorian pub where we were to meet, stepped around a large police horse wearing a visor (no kidding) and tried to fight my way through to the bar. I'd only got halfway when I became aware that the silence that had broken out around me was extremely similar to that I once experienced by turning into the Short Strand in Belfast with an English accent and a short back and sides haircut.

What had I done?

My path was blocked by what appeared to be a tattoo measuring 6 foot 6 by 4 foot and wearing a lot of black leather, and a scarf and woolly hat in colours that might as well have been those of Moscow Dynamo for all I knew. 'Evening, Officer,' it said. Aaah. Gotcha. It's the trench coat. This tattoo had seen Peter Falk as Columbo, and he knew as well as the rest of them how the plain-clothes filth always went about in trench coats, harassing ordinary blokes having a day out.

I simpered at him and fled.

I took off the trench coat, re-entered the pub with a crowd of people and nobody took a blind bit of notice of me, thank God.

Eventually we all walked down Loftus Road to the QPR ground, the bank manager's friend was suitably gobsmacked by being shown to a box, and the fun and games commenced. Before the first, or rather third, pre-lunch drink had been finished, a perfectly respectable stockbroker began to yell 'CMMAAAHNYEWIIIIIRRRRUUNNNNS' at the top of his voice. This, apparently, is an accepted West Ham warcry, but since it was still two hours before kick-off and we were behind a plate-glass window at the furthest corner of the pitch, I failed to see how it was going to achieve the desired motivational impact.

Lunch and drinks (and more drinks) proceeded and in due course the ground began to fill up and with half an hour to go it seemed to me that you couldn't have got an ectomorphic stick insect into any part of the terraces.

I discovered later that it was at about this point that another two thousand supporters came in at the far end of the pitch from us with the result that those already there were forced out onto the field where the Old Bill was not prepared to let them sit.

This meant that they were herded round the touch line to wherever the copper in charge decided that there was a bit of terrace insufficiently populated. Their ingress was stoutly resisted by those already in occupation (I guess they must have been the wrong sort of supporters), and the copper in charge was offered several suggestions, some of them accompanied by gestures, as to where he could put them, together with his police horse.

This exchange of witticisms resulted in police snatch squads charging into the crowd to weed out the disruptive elements, only to be followed by more coppers trying to find out what happened to the first lot.

Now this was all very entertaining stuff, but I thought I'd been brought along to have my prejudices shattered. While enjoying the spectacle, I offered my banking friend a fiver for every woman he could find in the crowd at this 'game for all the family'. There were none, or if there were, both he and I failed to spot them and my fiver remained in my wallet.

The kick-off was delayed for forty-five minutes, during which time a young woman working for the caterers came in and locked the booze away, listened to several raunchy suggestions from the stockbroker without appearing to be amused at all, then play started.

Then the booze cupboard was miraculously open and then play was stopped for another minor skirmish, and by the time it got to half-time, I had to go home to sort out the laundry.

By the middle of the following week my friend had received a substantial bill for damage to the box which, after accepting the Club's invitation to re-visit the scene, he paid without a murmur.

Aaaah well, a lad's entitled to a bit of fun after all that graft at work, and if it gets them out of the house it must be worth it, eh?

CHAPTER FIFTEEN

Suffer the Children . . .

'Insanity is hereditary . . . or heredity is insanitary . . . either way you get it from your children.'

ADJUSTED GRAFFITO

THE ONSET OF SUMMER MEANT I LEARNT A GREAT DEAL about housewormery *mit kindern*. This is very different, and a good deal more stressful, than poncing about with a feather duster while the offspring are out of the way getting educated.

I've been thinking about this a lot, and I've decided that the biggest shock to the average working Joe's system if he had to take up housewormery, would be the reality of dealing with his children on a twenty-four-hour basis. Working Dad the bank manager can have photographs of

his smiling wife and family clearly displayed on his desk so
that the poor supplicants may be fooled into thinking he's
human, and he may kiss them all sweetly as they troop up to
the bath before bed, and he may bring his sons guns and his
daughters dolls and take them all swimming on Saturdays,
but he has not a clue as to the true natures of his darling,
doted-on offspring.

Just after our second child was born, I was remarking
how nice the top of his head smelt . . . even the Siamese
cats thought so.

'It's a defence mechanism,' some smart aleck informed
me, 'it's so you like them and don't hurt them.'

What I want to know is what happened to this? By
the time the average child is two years old, the 'aren't I
magic and don't you love me?' aroma has given way to
something that gives out a stink more along the lines of
'C'mon, crumblies. Give it your best shot! Bet I can give
you a coronary before you can murder me.' Mothers know
this, and have been equipped with the sort of self-control
the Anger Management therapists would kill for. Fathers
have to be watched very carefully, since their self-control
tends more towards the John McEnroe school of action
and reaction.

Mostly this is because all children with siblings view their
sibs as the enemy, their parents as the UN and the home
as the war zone. And we all know how popular among the
combatants the UN can be.

By the middle of The Major Year, five-year-old Rosie's
chief interest was the well-being of her many babies, all
of whom had to be cared for by their grandfather (me,
apparently) while Rosie 'went shopping'. This sort of
magical world is pretty easy to live in, if you're five. If
you're forty-seven, the fun of telling their mother what
seven dolls had for their tea and whether they have been
bathed yet palls after the third or fourth repetition.

By the same time, Joe's principal delight in life was to pull
the rug out from under his sister's misconceptions. He's not

a vindictive bloke, but small sisters are not playmates, they are fair game.

By eight, Joe's age, adults have started to knock the glow off that world by the quaint old process known as education.

Riding on a wave of adult approval, and secure in the rightness of his newly acquired knowledge, Joe will say, 'Don't be silly, SHE's not a baby, she's a DOLL!'

Rosie will yell back, 'We're PRETENDING. And if we're PRETENDING, then she IS a baby.'

'No she's not. YOU'RE a BABY!!'

And let battle commence.

The correct answer to a five-year-old's query, 'What can jump higher than a house?' is NOT 'Just about anything, a house can't jump.'

The correct answer is, 'I don't know, what can jump higher than a house?' and let them do it. People who don't live with children (they may *have* children) don't understand this, and when their wives (usually) get cross with them for spoiling the five-year-old's gag, they honestly don't know what the hell she's on about.

They fight less, thank God, as they get older, but other factors intrude, like hero-worship, or the opposite sex, or acne . . . all of which, as any mother can tell you, can cause no fewer tears before bedtime than mere sibling rivalry.

The only thing that can unite these sibs is the discovery of something gross, or the need to put something over on their parents. We once came upon our two eldest sons, aged about six and four, and miraculously diverted from their perpetual internecine warfare, lying side by side on the floor of the bathroom closely examining the blood-soaked rear legs and tail that were all that remained of a squirrel that had encountered one of the Siamese and only come second.

'What is it?' the younger one asked his big brother, who read a lot.

'I think it was a squirrel or a rabbit but it's dead!'

'Mmm. What did it die of?'

The elder boy paused. 'I'm not QUITE sure, but I think it was a brain haemorrhage!'

I told you he read a lot.

What turned this diagnostician into 6 foot 3 of bare-footed, pony-tailed self-absorption, God only knows. Testosterone, probably. All undergraduate-age children have clearly divined that their mission in life is to stand about in contemplative heaps so as to block out the light in between bouts of emptying the fridge.

Ours are really nice, but what are they thinking about? I know all that Kahlil Gibran stuff about children 'dwelling in the land of tomorrow where we cannot go even in our dreams', but do they have to dwell in the land of tomorrow TODAY, especially when I'm trying to get lunch?

And do they have to loom over me and spread out the *Daily Mail* so I can't get at the cupboards? And why do they READ the *Daily Mail*? And why, when I ask Number One to get out two soup spoons and three small knives, do I have to ask three times in ascending volume levels before he says, 'Mmmm? Oh, sorry,' and hands me three soup spoons, two knives and four forks?

Why, when I lose my cool and yell, 'OUT! Clear off! Get lost! I'll call when lunch is ready!' does Number Two look up and say, 'WOW! Stresssyyyy, dude!'? Now this MAY make me laugh, but don't count on it. He counts on it, and if it doesn't he says, 'Oh, gurrhrate!' and takes himself off to his room in a sulk.

It's this clown who teaches Joe all the Newman and Baddiel lines, so that my infrequent witticisms or attempts thereat are greeted by eight-year-old sighs of 'Oooh, like . . . er . . . har, har . . . I mean . . . like . . . giggle.'

Back to insanitary.

It has taken six months as a Houseworm for me to divine the origin and provenance of the following term of abuse: 'You're just an old woman.'

It conjures up, does it not, a picture of someone per-
nickety, uptight, resentful and well past their sell-by date,
whose principal areas of concern are trivial matters that the
movers and shakers have too strategic a view to concern
themselves with.

I will tell you how she got to BE 'an old woman', this
person, and how, eventually, I got to be one, too.

Mrs Neanderthal, her of the rock hyrax stew, once she
had decided to let her husband get on with the trivia like
dealing with Sabre-tooth PLC while she concentrated on
the really important things like seeing their children were
properly fed and the cave was kept warm and Mr N. got
his from time to time, also decided that, boys being boys,
he would need to feel that what he did was the serious stuff,
so she let him.

She even convinced him of it by simpering a lot and
telling him what a powerful and important mover and
shaker he was, and being the dumb sonofabitch he was,
he believed her.

This worked very well for a time, what with him coming
home pooped and needing to be told how great he was
and that boss of his, Mr Cretaceous, was nothing but an
old meanie, and if he had any sense the company would
be called Neanderthal, Sabre-tooth & Associates.

This made Mr N. feel better and a lot more important,
and probably horny as well, so the pair of them never got
around to what sort of a day *she'd* had, and there's nothing
for giving old N an attack of the wilts like telling him about
Neanderthal junior's tonsillitis, so she didn't.

After a couple of decades of this, Mr N. and the kids, both
male and female, have learnt that what the by-now-getting-
on-for-middle-aged woman does isn't important enough to
bother with, right?

After all, for thirty years it hasn't been important enough
to talk about, whereas Old Cretaceous' son-in-law's golf
handicap, why that's all Dad's been talking about for
weeks. Ever since the son-in-law won the Jurassic Pro-am

and Cretaceous stopped speaking to Dad and passed him over for promotion, again.

By this time, Mr N. and the kids have all ceased to notice who cooks, cleans, washes, clears up and does the laundry, because nobody ever mentions it, but by now Mrs N. is beginning to think she may have been a bit too clever for her own good, and she's getting pretty pissed off at still picking up after the lot of them, and scrubbing the bowl of the latrine after them, and taking the crunchy hanky out of Mr N.'s bearskin where he's thrown it on the floor every night for thirty years, and cooking rock hyrax stew only to find that not even this can prevent Mr N.'s by now permanent wilts, and never having any of them offer to HELP.

After all, who could need help with something so trivial as housewormery, right?

Finally, she goes ape. The cave becomes filled with 'Wipe your feet how many times do I have to tell you if you leave your bones on the workslab again I'm throwing them out you hear me and I've just cleaned that floor and if you want your clothes washed put them in the laundry hole for a change and at nineteen I think you could be expected to make your own ledge don't you and do your homework and don't play with your food and if you don't care for rock hyrax stew any more that's tough buddy because frankly I don't care for carrying on dealing with you ungrateful, insensitive, inconsiderate, arrogant, self-important CREEPS for one more day', and then HE says, 'Aaaah. Change of life, is it?'

See? She's now 'an old woman', fussing about trivia, and THAT's how she got to be one.

Believe me, you don't have to be female.

My bank manager friend says he couldn't look after kids; he hasn't got the patience. (This is from a West Ham supporter!) What every woman knows, or at least those who have kids, is that it's the looking after that produces the patience.

Macho Mike's idea of looking after the kids while his

wife pops round to her mother's of a Saturday afternoon is, now that they've rebelled against having to watch rugby, to invest in three or four videos he considers educational, like *Top Gun* and *Terminator 2*, and plonk the boys in front of the TV in the sitting-room for the afternoon. He then goes up to the bedroom and watches the Calcutta Cup on his own. When his wife gets home and raises her eyes to heaven and says, 'Honestly! You think that's spending time with your children?', he doesn't know what she's wittering on about, and worse, he says so. A few months as a Houseworm, and even Mike would know about quality time. Being responsible ALL the time sure puts the guilt on the gingerbread.

You know about home being 'the place that when you go there they have to take you in'?

Well, kids are like employees who will never resign and you're not allowed to sack.

They SAY they want to resign often enough. Joe, prompted by Calvin, frequently points out that my position in the polls is even worse than that of the Prime Minister and when am I coming up for re-election? It is a profound source of disappointment to him to be informed that I have tenure for life.

Then he says am I going to be doing the cooking and the school run for much longer because he thinks I'm OK as DAD, it's just that other boys have proper mums, and he feels silly. HE feels silly? Rosie says, 'All children love their mummy more than their daddy because they just do, that's why.'

Where do they get this extremely non-PC attitude? Imbibed with mother's milk, no doubt, along with all the preconceptions that only need a friend's mother to reinforce them.

Rosie had long been refusing to go round to her friend Lucy's to play unless one of her parents went with her. Having played this adult gooseberry game throughout her fifth year (I simply refuse to join in another game of 'The Farmer's in his Den'), we decided that if she was invited to go to a friend's, she could, but she'd be on her own.

(It occurs to me that the pressure from *Woman's Hour*-listening mothers would be the other way. If she had a friend round, they would need to be accompanied so that I could be supervised.)

Finally, she said she'd go to Lucy's. Now I don't know about other blokes doing this job (what other blokes?), but I am sometimes led to remonstrate with my dear wife about her tendency to cross-examine our younger children's friends on such matters as what their fathers do and does their mother work and do they have any brothers or sisters and what time do they get up in the morning and what do they have for breakfast and why does she want to KNOW all this stuff?

Anyway, Lucy's mother has the same party trick. When I arrive to collect Rosie, a bit anxious that her hostess has been led a long and tearful dance all afternoon, I am immediately confronted by a list of my inadequacies as a mother.

'Rosie says you sometimes cook,' she tells me, 'but that mostly you burn things ... Never mind, you're a man, after all.'

'What things?' I enquire indignantly of a by now increasingly embarrassed Rosie.

'I'll tell you at home,' she says.

Lucy's mother leans over. 'You don't want to be shy, Rosie. Burning supper is what daddies do, isn't it. They can't help it. It's because they're boys and they don't know about cooking, do they?'

By now I'm beginning to think that what we have here is a clear case of the witness giving the answers she knows the prosecutor wishes to hear, and I'm just getting around to wondering what other gems of misinformation have been gravely handed over as gospel truth, when Rosie indicates that she wishes to go home NOW!

That evening after supper (cooked by me and uncharacteristically carbon-free), the wife and mother calls from Manchester and Rosie is desperate to talk to her.

I put her on.

'Daddy, go away!'

'Wha'?'

'Daddeee, I want to tell Mummy a secret! Go away!'

What can anyone do? So off I go, and a whispered conversation ensues, followed some hours later by the breadwinner's return.

'Want to know what that was all about, do you?' she asks.

'You betcha.'

'She had a wee [I use the word advisedly] lavatorial accident at Lucy's, and she wanted me to put her knickers in the laundry so you wouldn't see.'

(!)

Don't ask me, madam, I just work here.

It was always my contention, long before I was washed up on this rocky shore, that what children get up to in their own rooms need not concern their parents. As long as they are prepared to live in said rooms in the conditions prevailing, and expect no-one else to tidy up, clear up or pick up, then they are on their own and can live as they wish. This, as I say, was before Houseworm's eye (and nose) brought home to me the full extent of the horrors that our children not only endure, but which, apparently, form the sort of surroundings that they consider essential for the modern bedroom.

It is not just the clothes, or the books, or the toys, or the comics, or the bedclothes, or the Coke tins, or the week-old cups of cold tea, or the musical instruments, or the cassettes, or the ghetto-blaster or even the now useless felt-tips with their lids off. It is the fact all these items are on the floor, and the drawers, bookshelves and cupboards provided are empty or contain (in the case of sons one and two) inadequately concealed ashtrays and the half-bottle of rum I couldn't find last week, or (in Joe's case) the two enormous plastic buckets formerly containing twenty years' accumulation of Lego bits which now lie ankle-deep from wall to wall.

Another thing: one day Houseworms, housewives and other domestic wildlife will form an alliance and every toy manufacturer from Lego to Matchbox will be forced to spend eternity picking up the hundreds of tiny pieces which go to make up any given product. Their distributors will be condemned for a similar period to walk barefoot, in desperate need of a lavatory, in the dark, over a landing completely covered in the sharpest bits of Lego and the most jagged possessions of Polly Pocket.

Anyone (like me for instance) who doesn't understand the intricacies of Chaos Theory or the subtler workings of the physics of entropy has no hope whatsoever of understanding the Houseworm Theory of Relativity.

This states that no matter how quickly you clean or tidy a room, one or more of your relatives can return it to a condition considerably worse than that prevailing before you started in less than one tenth of the time.

Judge for yourself: I start after breakfast in the left-hand corner of the kitchen with cloth, Marigolds, cleaner/disinfectant spray and a sink full of hot water. I spray and wipe surfaces and tiles and draining-boards and cupboard doors and the top and front of the Aga (and polish the lids) and underneath the toaster and the microwave and inside and outside the back door which the dog opens himself so it's got mud on it to a height of 5, no 6, feet, and then the sides, tops and fronts of the fridge and the freezer and the door of the larder.

To do this I put (or throw) away two perfectly good boxes of tissues the cats have taken to nesting in, eleven small toys, three large toys (a tricycle is required furniture for a work surface apparently), two boxes of felt-tips (I'm not using HIS colours!), one squash racket, an old yellow *Travel Show* script, the first twenty-two pages of which have, on the reverse, twenty-two identical pictures of a princess with golden hair standing under a rainbow next to a house with flowers at the front and a tree in the yard, all of which Rosie and her mother consider to be a vital record of her artistic development which must NOT be thrown away; and the homework that Joe said he couldn't find before he left for school and thirteen conkers, four of which have string through them, and the detritus formed by boring out the holes for the string, and the Househead's post from today and yesterday which are easily distinguishable because yesterday's letters have been opened and then returned to their envelopes and been left exactly where she found them, which is where today's letters now are.

Why keep the envelopes?

And I fold today's papers and also move her mobile phone battery charger and the pot that contains clothes-brush and hairbrush for last-minute adjustments to pre-school children.

Once this has been done I pull out all the chairs from the kitchen table and wipe and disinfect them and remove the cat and dog hairs from their feet and invert them on the table and then I open the cupboard under the sinks where the compost, rubbish and chicken buckets live and breed, and clear all that out and scrape the crud off the inner doors, floors and walls where we chucked stuff in and missed, and empty and disinfect the buckets and put in new bin-bags, and then I sweep the floor. Then I mop the floor. Then I polish the floor.

Then it's lunch-time. Don't time fly?

By the time Son One has had lunch the work surfaces have acquired two literary critiques of Browning, his wallet (Son One's, not Browning's) and an undergraduate's guide to the dreaming spires; and today's papers are on top of the toaster in a heap.

At four o'clock Joe and Rosie get out of the car and by the time I get into the house, the kitchen worktops contain two school blazers, one cardigan, one pair of trainers, one pair of very muddy football boots, two satchels, six conkers (none with string in), four micro-men warriors in various stages of undress, three exercise books, two school newsletters, one pile of cat sick and a partridge in a bloody pear tree.

Then the Househead comes home and opens her post.

See? It's not the children that drive you mad . . . well, it's not *just* the children.

CHAPTER SIXTEEN
Interlude

'Dulling, you're soooo clever! What a lovely dress; I just can't wait for them to come back into fashion again!'

AUNT EVIE TO MY MUM

THE SOCIAL WHIRL PROVIDES ANOTHER FASCINATING facet on the jewel of housewormery. When UT and Evie lived near by, I was briefly seconded to housework as a sort of part-time training programme before taking up my full-time duties last year.

Picture this: it's six-thirty on a Wednesday evening and I'm knackered. The Househead's away doing telly, the sons one and two are likewise, doing education, and the smalls are in the middle of supper and a fight.

The phone rings: 'Dulling, you MUST come across and

escort me. Toby's away somewhere, I forget where, and those nice people next door, you know the ones, with the dogs, no, the other dogs, silly boy . . . I don't know their names, dulling, they've just invited us to supper and they've got what'sisname, you know, on the telly, coming, and it could be a great help in your career. You know the one who does that show with the lights.' *Countdown? Blockbusters?*

'How should I know, dulling, you know I never watch the dreadful telly. Can you come? You must, I need a man, dulling. Wear a suit or something.'

It has long since been brought home to me that it's absolutely no good telling Evie that my acting career, such as it was, is over and goodoh, say I. She has been convinced ever since we first met that I was going to be the Olivier of the Eighties (look out, Branagh), and thus introduce her to the world to which she feels she had to forfeit her claim by marrying UT at the ripe old age of eighteen before she could even audition for RADA.

Evie was brought up in an age where young ladies were expected to be highly decorative and slightly dizzy and simper a lot in the presence of their heroic menfolk who were either sorting out the colonies or the Boche and had home fires that needed to be kept burning.

This may have been cute at eighteen, but in an extremely beady lady of sixty-wotsis it comes across a bit hollow. But fifty years of UT would make Saddam Hussein simper to order.

'Evie, don't be daft, you don't need me, just go! I'm a wife and mother, remember? I've got responsibilities.'

Five minutes later Pam comes in from her cottage. 'Evie says I have to babysit while you go out with her!' Pam is one of those mothers-in-law who make Bernard Manning look paranoid. She's a pushover. She'll do anything for anyone without even being asked and she's no match for Evie's avalanche of 'dullings'.

I hand over smalls, leave instructions about not only bathing but washing,* and leave the mother-in-law with a large G&T and instructions to ignore all bleats from upstairs after 8 p.m.

(* NB!! Towards an understanding of BATH-TIME: Notoriously unreliable, and prone to amnesia, small children are invariably involved in an experiment to discover how much supper needs to adhere to the cheeks, eyebrows and ears before the weight of food detritus stretches the facial tissue as far as the navel. They are loath to have this important experiment terminated and the Househead does not approve of placing them naked in the garage and turning the fire-hose on them. There has, therefore, to be a regular period of prolonged physical contact involving water, soap, flannel, nail-brush, patent felt-tip and ball-pen ink remover and dandruff shampoo. This last to be alternated with anti-nit lotion, for among the mathematical achievements, letters, pictures, flower arrangements, jellies, small and reluctant 'best friends' and biscuits made from Cocopops that children bring home from school, there are colds, flu, viruses and contagious diseases including, for all the Houseworm knows, AIDS. The most persistent of these doubtful prizes is headlice, which have been specially bred to boost the sales of the chemical companies who manufacture the foul-smelling shampoos/lotions that are guaranteed to eliminate the problem right up to the point when the child gets back to school. The only immediate benefit of the lotion is that while applying it it is impossible to smell either of the older children.)

I digress.

Evie has no children of her own, provided you don't count UT, and her way of dealing with *him* is to ignore him. She's the only person on earth who can do this, and after UT has expended a great deal of energy and malice trying to put her down, he finds it tough when her only reply is to ask him to pay the newspaper bill. At family lunch she sits schtum throughout, but as soon as UT's out of the way there's no stopping her.

I get to their house ten minutes later to find Evie pouring

the whole of a bottle of rather nasty South African brandy (a gift to UT, no doubt, from a grateful customer) into a large bowl of dried prunes. Evie's household management is a monument to intestinal regularity in which prunes play a significant part. Perhaps this accounts for UT's manners.

'Hullo, what's up?'

'Ooooh, dulling, I'm not ready yet, you see, this is for pudding, see, and I thought it would be delicious to let the prunes soak up the brandy because I promised I'd bring them something and prunes and brandy seem to be all that there is in the house. Toby's out all the time, and I hardly eat anything, as you know, so do you think this will be all right?'

I'm too gobsmacked to care.

I don't yet know what I'm doing here, and now I'm expected to adjudicate on the idea of half-dried plums in a sauce that's 40 per cent proof.

We set out for dinner with Evie's pudding sloshing about on the back seat and 'those people next door' turn out to live at the other end of the village and the supper to which we have been invited turns out to be a black-tie dinner given by some ex-captain of industry who extended the invitation in the vain belief that UT's influence extends to getting him, if not a knighthood, at least a place among the great and the good.

Only UT could have given him this idea.

Neither he nor his wife have ever met Evie (*she* only recognizes *them* because of the dogs) and were certainly not expecting *me*, dressed as I am in a suit which I last wore when I was two stone lighter and which now requires me to hold my stomach in to an extent that makes my eyes look as though I have a thyroid problem.

Evie is unfazed.

'Hulloo, dulling, you're just sooo sweet to ask us, you know Toby's nephew-in-law, don't you, and I've brought you some pudding which you must put somewhere where it can soak up its juice. Oh look, dulling, there are your divine dogs,' and she's off down the corridor leaving her hostess holding a sticky glass-bowl and wondering if the village has acquired a mad bag-lady that no-one's told her about.

Me, I'm beginning to realize that I would be a lot happier in my own bathroom trying to get Biro off Joe's eyebrows with a nail-brush.

My hostess is still opening and shutting her mouth without any audible effect, so I explain who I am and we gather up Evie from among the mêlée of animals in the kitchen (where the couple of extremely dishy young women who are catering this bash do not appear overwhelmed by Evie's contribution to the dessert trolley but feign enthusiasm) and in we go.

Our host is a sort of UT Mk II who visibly swells with indignation at the sight of my shiny suit but is quickly informed that I'm *in loco* UT and therefore un-chuckoutable.

He lavishes attention on Evie, however, who is quick to inform him that although UT's away, 'he wouldn't have come anyway, dulling, he's such a bore, isn't he. Now me, dulling, I just had to see your gorgeous dogs, so I brought Penny's husband to keep me company, he's an actor, you know.'

'Oh, really? What have you done?'

Oh boy.

'Recently just a few local readings, I'm afraid.'

I mean, this geek should catch my nightly evocation, complete with sound effects, of *The BFG* for a spellbound audience of two.

'Huhnh? Can't be much good if you don't get jobs, huhnh?'

This interrogative 'huhnh?', I rapidly discover, is tacked onto the end of every sentence this old boy utters, and it means, 'With me, so far? Paying attention, are you? Grasped the essential wisdom of my position? Weren't thinking of interrupting, were you?'

I'm thinking of asking him if he'd be prepared to hire it

out to UT as it would make a change from 'see, boy?' but
it's apparent he needs it pretty much full time. He takes me
aside and says he may be able to effect an introduction for
me, seeing I'm a relation of UT's, because the finest actress
in Britain, and her film producer husband, are among
the guests.

These turn out to be two people I've never heard of, but
they must be in the business since they spend the entire
time they're talking to me peering over my shoulder to see
if they can spot someone more interesting, or possibly just
someone ELSE.

It subsequently turns out that he owns an independent
production company (after the ITV franchise round and
Birt's arrival at the Beeb, who doesn't?) and she, leading
lady of the British Theatre, has a running part in a day-time
soap and once did a nurse in *Casualty*. This, come to think
of it, is more than I've done, so I stop referring to her as
Maggie Smith and try to behave.

We sit down to dinner and Evie, to my delight, gets to
sit next to the film producer.

'Now, dulling. You simply MUST tell me all about yourself. You see my escort over there? That's my nephew-in-law
and he's really a wonderful actor. Resting, at the moment,
such a bore, don't you agree . . . there must be something
he could do for you, dulling, there simply must be.'

I quickly interrupt to tell Evie she's embarrassing me and
explain that even if I were offered a part as an extra in the
Halifax commercial I would be unable to do it due to other
commitments.

'Oh, yeah? What?' says Hollywood's finest, who clearly
thinks I ought to be more grateful for the two milliseconds
he's spent even considering my far from obvious potential.

Here we go.

If there's one thing likely to be more embarrassing than
a discussion of my acting triumphs it's the revelation of my
present occupation.

Evie was never embarrassed in her life. 'He's the most

wonderful man, dulling. Wonderful. He even looks after the children.'

For the childless Evie the joys of children are so obscure that she views childcare as something you are reduced to when you lose your job cleaning sewers.

'OHMIGOD,' shrieks Dame Maggie. 'You're not a NEW MAN, or something?'

'Or something,' say I, this being one of my more guarded moments.

'What a scream!' she says, and turns to Norman Jewison. 'Do you hear that, sweetie? Bet you couldn't even boil an egg.' (You mean she doesn't KNOW?)

The film director mutters that if God had meant him to look after his children He'd have given him tits.

The lady thinks this is pretty sexist stuff, and by the time the pudding comes round the whole table is involved in an increasingly acrimonious discussion about domestic responsibilities, feminism and patriarchal role attitudes.

I manage, for once, to keep my mouth shut and remain grateful that they've all forgotten that it was my lifestyle that got this whole can of worms open in the first place.

When the pudding arrives, the catering ladies have decided that Evie's offering should be given pride of place, and round they come with the by now bloated prunes and a bowl of whipped cream that smells extremely strongly of Kirsch. I wisely decline after hearing Evie refuse her own creation by saying she had prunes for breakfast 'and enough's as good as a feast, isn't it, dulling?'

Not one of the other eight guests, including the local doctor who ought to know better, refuses this brown bowel-bomb, and as the first prune-full spoonfuls go down, the guests' final shreds of sobriety vanish like mist. The whole table starts to talk rubbish as if under some Bacchanalian spell, with our host by now promising everyone 'Rather good brandy, huhnh? Or port, huhn?' from the stocks on the sideboard as he unwittingly spoons another ⅓ gill in with the next prune, and the actress remarking apropos of God knows what that people who don't understand how a woman feels are usually lousy in bed, and the two stunning (and likewise stunned) caterers looking round the table trying to work out what the hell they've done, when Evie suddenly declares that she's had a lovely time, dulling, but she really must get home in case Toby gets back and wonders where she is because 'you know he'll never feed his own dogs, don't you, dulling.'

We are out of there, clutching our newly washed glass pudding bowl, without anyone round the dinner table even noticing.

'Bye,' we said; 'Thank you,' we said; but all we heard was the actress, like Jennifer Saunders on uppers, saying, 'P'raps if you COULD boil an egg, sweetie, you'd know something of how a woman feels!', and the director looking at both of the catering ladies and saying, 'I bloody KNOW how a woman feels, b'lieve me, harhar', and our host saying, 'Brandy, huhnh? Good sauce with those prunes, huhnh? Don't know how these girls do it, huhnh?'

I think the doctor was asleep.

I drove Evie home. Carefully.

'Don't know what came over them all, dulling, really I don't. Do you? Silly man should give you a job, dulling, but he started to talk gibberish and then I got tired. It was all that having to make a pudding, it was ridiculous. Imagine how cross Toby would have been if he'd been there, you know how he likes people to listen when he talks, and none of them listened at all, did you notice?'

I dropped her outside her front door and watched her walk in. Toby had returned during our evening out, and I saw the bedroom light go on. I left before the old bugger could come down and make my life even more stressful. Evie's much better at dealing with him. I think it must be the prunes.

CHAPTER SEVENTEEN

Vive la Différence

'Today's woman is wittier, more worldly and certainly more glamorous than her husband.'

A.A. GILL in the *Daily Telegraph*

I COULD TELL THE MOMENT THE ABOVE *BONS MOTS* MET my bleary eyes from between the Alpen, Joe's satchel and the marmalade on the breakfast table that this day was not going to be a good one.

I decided to save my blood pressure for later, and started yelling about how we were going to be late for school and why hadn't they cleaned their teeth and where was Joe's homework and Rosie's reading-book and why didn't they listen to a word I said and now brush your hair and where's your school hat?

After all these months I can now do this while making myself a slice of toast, pouring myself coffee, kicking the dog's head out of the chicken bucket and reading the front page of the newspaper.

Further, it is not necessary to know what the time IS to know that you are running late, so the above diatribe can be delivered on an *ad hoc* basis at any time between dawn and departure. If it is not true at this precise moment, it very soon will be, and I can think of myself in the same terms as those high-fliers who get into corporate headquarters before the cleaning staff in order to steal a march on the day.

On this particular morning the only hiccup occurs half-way to school in the pouring rain and two miles of stationary traffic. 'Oh NO!' Joe says. 'WOT?' says I.

'You forgot that letter you have to sign about the school outing.'

Note the ease with which eight years of experience can unload full responsibility for everything from school documents to unseasonable weather on forty-seven years of thinking they're probably right.

Not this time.

'Look, bozo,' I tell him, 'if you'd even TOLD me about this letter, let alone shown it to me, I might hold still for this early-morning guilt trip, but this is the first time you've mentioned it, so don't come the raw prawn with me, sport. This is strictly your problem.'

'No it's not! You're supposed to go through my satchel to see if there's anything important . . . that's what Mum says.'

'Aha. Is this supposed to be done while you settle in front of *Roadrunner* with two pints of Alpen and a cockatiel in your cereal bowl?'

'Mmm. An' Mum says you have to do it because you're a crumbly and I'M COOL!'

The knowledge that the better half was not available the previous evening to put her domestic duty theory into practice, which would have resulted in the letter, if it existed, being now drawing-pinned to the cork board by the telephone for my attention when, by telepathy presumably, I'd divined that it needed it, means it is PROBABLY STILL IN HIS SATCHEL!

'OK, Joe,' I say. 'I can solve your problem because it is I, not you, who is cool. You say the letter's in your satchel? So open your satchel and get it out and I'll sign it, OK?'

God, the microscopic triumphs that make up the peaks in a Houseworm's day. Ninety-nine times out of a hundred the letter WOULD have been pinned to the wall at home either because herself had decided to help out or because Joe had only remembered to tell me about it after the 9 p.m. red-wine cut-off point, when I would have happily pinned it up myself, feeling highly organized and virtuous, and forgotten it, along with every single item on the nine o'clock news, by 6 a.m. this morning.

However, I float home on a wave of self-satisfaction at not having exposed myself to 'The Look' from Joe's teacher, who, if she is not doing Mrs Attila impressions, is nice but beady.

I ruminate, as I drive, on our family's collective ability to use any sort of filing system as an excuse for not actually doing anything. 'Take no action,' we say. 'You can always file it!' We all do this, because now the Househead's womanly methods have taken over.

Talking of womanly methods, it has been brought to my attention that the reason very few women tell jokes is that they realize how USELESS jokes are. Most jokes are irrelevant, and only a man can work up an interest in 'two elephants and a crocodile walking into a bar and the first elephant says . . .' where a woman knows this has no bearing on real life, and ceases to pay attention. Rosie calls jokes 'LIES' and won't have anything to do with them. Perhaps jokes fill up the space in the male consciousness left vacant by their lack of a constant awareness of children and domesticity.

Time was when I was efficient; dangerous, even.

Incoming paperwork would be dealt with, and once dealt

with, binned. A course of action in my business days that frequently led to trouble with suppliers whose invoice I had binned without, they claimed, actually dealing with it. Well, certainly not to the extent of issuing a cheque. Anyway, once I'd learnt to file stuff that HAD been dealt with, I had proof of action.

The wife has proof of everything except action. She has never thrown away a piece of paper in her life, and for years I couldn't understand why the fattest file in her office contained items filed under T.

'What's all that stuff under T?'

She gave me a pitying look.

'Things to Do,' she said.

Now we all file things like her, not in order to be able to demonstrate the action we have taken, but in order to avoid acting at all. The eldest son gets a bank statement, the second son gets an invitation to join a golf club, the wife gets a fan letter asking for a pic, and three years later I find them filed neatly in the kitchen bookshelf between Delia Smith and Sarah Brown.

I have an IN-tray and an OUT-tray for domestic admin. The Househead has an IN-tray only. She once asked me what I needed two trays of stuff for. I explained. She said, 'Jeeez, really?' and went back to see if the bottom document in her single tray dated from before we had children.

But now, eight months after starting on this precarious and original course, the siren song of procrastination has got me, and I'm pre-filing, rather than post-filing, with the best of them.

My brain must be beginning to take on that scatter-gun, feminine ability to concentrate on six things at once and file them all for attention at some later date while I get on with getting the supper.

When I get home the paper is waiting, along with that cup of coffee I shouldn't have, and the stuff about women being wittier, worldlier and more glamorous than their husbands means that there is NO WAY the fridge is getting defrosted this morning.

APPARENTLY (according to A.A. Gill, no less), there is a condition known as 'Smart Women Foolish Choices' or SWFC syndrome. This is where high-powered, intelligent and (according to the sexist Gill) attractive women marry dorks (his word not mine, for fairly obvious reasons). Apparently they do this with the result that when Mr and Mrs Gill go out to dinner he gets to sit between two stunning women, either of whom could be considered for the next Head of the United Nations, while SHE gets to sit between their two wimpish husbands whose idea of a good time is a day spent with extruded plastic mouldings and evenings playing Dungeons and Dragons.

WHY they marry berks they are falling over themselves to explain to good old AA. They do it because they like the hurly-burly of intellectual stimulation and competitive point-scoring during working hours, but when they come home they want good old Dorky offering a safe haven with no danger of argument or competition.

Subsequently, of course, Dorky bores the knickers off them and they find stimulation, physical and mental, elsewhere.

This leads to divorce; at which point A.A. Gill turns up and asks why they married such a berk in the first place and THEY say: 'SWFC syndrome, darling.'

Alongside this is another piece suggesting that women over fifty would much rather be talking to children or dogs than the author who has been seated next to them at dinner, and that's why he'd much rather be seated next to someone young and stimulating, and, if he's lucky, pretty, who will treat any mention of children or animals with the contempt it deserves, and regale him with witty and urbane banter about really important things like Tory MPs' sex lives and the London Interbank Overnight Rate.

Apart from the idea that it might be interesting to hear what these writers' dinner companions think of *them*, it occurs to me that what we have here is a double bind . . . people who stay at home and raise families are only fit to converse with dogs and children, and people who are safe, secure and non-competitive are dorks who entirely lack any intellectual capacity such as might stimulate old AA's lady over dinner.

By the time I've stacked the dishwasher, I'm in danger of agreeing with these two pillocks.

'Is that what I am?' I start asking myself. 'My particular smart woman's foolish choice? If I'm not, how did I get to be a Houseworm? Psychologically, I mean. Am I one of A.A. Gill's dorks, and if so WHY DON'T I MIND?'

OK, Dr Freud, listen up.

My father died when I was thirteen years old, and the following Christmas my mother (What? Oh yes, Doc, a *very* strong character) took my sister (yup, another one and a serious achiever, to boot) and myself to Austria to spend Christmas with an extremely old Austrian gentleman, head of some corporation or other, who had formed a close friendship with my father despite the fact that he spoke not more than two words of English and my father spoke no German at all.

Their communication was limited to lip-smacking appreciation of all that Austria or South Africa had to offer in the way of food and drink, and an ability to tell each other jokes, even in their respective language, without giving amusement, comprehension or offence to the hearer, but allowing the teller to laugh uproariously when he got to his own punchline.

We arrived on a train, late at night, at a tiny village which it seemed the old boy practically owned, to be greeted by a Germanic growl of 'Leiths?' from the darkness beyond the track (there was no platform).

For the next three days he drove us about in an extremely old Mercedes such as Goering may have been ferried about in, to various functions that the villagers had clearly been press-ganged into laying on for the benefit of his guests.

A succession of groaning tables met our exhausted and sated gaze, and at most of them we sipped mulled wine politely and watched Alf eat. This was something he did with a dedication and enthusiasm that showed no signs of flagging, no matter how many households had already shared their '*Gruss Gott*' and their supper with him. This parade culminated, on Christmas Eve, in what he was pleased to describe as 'MY MUSICKS'.

He had been pretty excited about 'MY MUSICKS' from the night we arrived, but the language problem and his obvious wish to surprise us, gave us no clue as to what we were in for.

Eventually, after a very long evening, we found out.

First Alf single-handedly consumed an entire carp at his daughter-in-law's house. Then they switched off the lights and opened the sliding doors to their sitting-room and my sister burst into tears at the beauty of the Christmas tree with real candles flickering in the dark, and we had to try to explain to our bemused hostess that she was, in fact, crying because she was HAPPY.

Then we attended Midnight Mass in a chapel on an alp of indescribable moonlit beauty where each gravestone had a flickering candle on it and the temperature inside differed from that outside only insofar as we were not actually kneeling on snow.

Just as we began to think we were about to go to bed where we could massage the smile-induced cramp out of our cheeks, we were taken to a room attached to the village hall that couldn't have been more than 20 feet square.

Half of it was taken up by a table containing every alcoholic beverage known to man, and the other half by all twenty-four members of the village brass band. These oompah merchants were Alf's 'MUSICKS' and four seats were arranged for us about 16 inches from the mouth of the nearest tuba. (There were several tubas, I seem to recall.)

Now they played and Alf drank and shouted instructions

and every number ended with '*Gut, ja?*' and our increasingly exhausted nods of inaudible enthusiasm spurred the players on to more schnapps and yet another (longer) series of mind-shattering oompahs.

At about three in the morning, toasts having been drunk to everyone present and celebrated in music and song, my mother finally cracked.

She somehow found the German for 'If you don't take us back to the hotel I'll burn the Reichstag again', and we weaved off, Alf at the wheel, into the starry, snowy Christmas-card night.

When we got to the hotel, Alf got, we thought, a pretty perfunctory good night and happy Christmas from our mother before she determinedly set off for bed.

At this point Alf reversed the off-side rear wheel of his car into a storm drain and sat in a stupor gunning the engine with his wheels spinning hopelessly.

The entire village had seized the opportunity provided by my mother's desire for sleep to escape Alf's enthusiasm for Christmas and get to bed themselves, so Prue and I stood about pushing feebly at the Merc's mudguards while Alf gunned the motor and bellowed imprecations out of the window.

After some moments my mother returned to find out what all the noise was about. Without a word she seized the rear bumper and lifted the back of the car single-handedly out of the drain, dropped it, and the spinning wheels gripped on the snow and Alf shot off down the hill like a torpedo and was halfway to Innsbruck before he knew what had happened.

We turned, gobsmacked, to a woman whose rage and exhaustion clearly gave her the strength of Godzilla and said, 'Presents now, Mum. It's Christmas!'

She said, 'Bugger Christmas,' and went to bed.

Since then 'Christmassy' means exactly the opposite, in our family, to what you might expect it to mean, and I reckon it's that sort of demonstration of female dominance experienced during my most formative and impressionable years, that made me think having women in charge was a pretty good wheeze. What do you think, *Herr Doktor*?

Not that the wife's 'in charge', you understand. 'Course not. I mean who's responsible for all this stuff? It's just that we have different methods, OK? It goes like this: I am making supper for the smalls when she comes down from her office to go to the loo and get herself another cup of tea. As she walks through the kitchen she says, 'Oh!' That's all, just 'Oh!'

My polite response comes out more as a shriek of 'WHAT??!!' than my super-cool self-image would like, and she says, 'Oh, nothing. It's just that there are those mashed potatoes and I thought you could use them and the left-over lentil dish from Tuesday to make them a pie. Then you could have used up the grated carrot in a salad. They like grated carrot. Never mind.'

Then she goes back up to her office, before I can tell her that I considered that particular option in detail and, after considerable thought, decided against it and in favour of the omelette they are now eating. As a matter of fact, she goes back to her office before I can even invent this lie.

Bet she never says 'Oh!' to the Prime Minister. 'I just thought you could have used that interest rate decision to get rid of the Chancellor. Never mind.'

Now there are, I admit, occasions on which she is ahead of me, but that's 'cos she's programmed that way. She's not bossy, interfering or supervisory, really. She just has to know what her children are being given to eat, wear or endure or she can't sleep nights. Me, I hand them over, and by the time I'm out of the drive if someone yelled 'Rosie' in my ear I'd say 'Who?' And I do not, on my return, enquire as to how much of what each small had consumed for supper, and whether they finished their homework.

If, by some miracle, I notice at 6.30 a.m. that we have more milk than we need and I'd better leave a note for Milko before he doubles it, I'll get outside to find that between returning from some TV studio at midnight and coming to bed, the helpmeet has already clocked this and the note's been written and is already nestling in the crate outside. She's not interfering, honest. Just helping. So why aren't I a lot more grateful and a lot less chippy?

I can tell you, given notice, when the smalls are due for a dental check-up. She can tell you, off the top of her head, the dates of all four children's next hygienist's appointment, dental check-up, half-term and the dates and opening hours of the school's second-hand uniform shop. While doing all this she can also tell you more about the Prime Minister than you might wish to know.

Having borne children gives her that joke-free extra level of awareness that covers hearth and home, and which cannot be obliterated by even the most severe concentration on some other matter. Me, I only have to concentrate on sweeping the floor in order to entirely forget that the children have homework to do and the guinea-pig hasn't been fed.

She has NEVER forgotten to collect them from school.

BUT . . . tadaah! After eight months of housewormery, she was in charge one evening because I'd been out; playing tennis probably. I came home to find her rolling out pastry and generally getting in an uproar. 'What do?' was my polite enquiry. 'What does it look like?' her less polite response. 'I'm making your ruddy supper.'

I paused, I savoured the moment. 'Didn't you look in the larder? I made us moussaka before I went out. I told Joe to tell you.' Hah!

She looked at me. 'It's no good asking Joe, men never remember anything. Next time tell Rosie.'

It only took me twenty minutes to get the pastry out of my hair, too.

Finally, Doctor, there's the driving bit. My friend Macho Mike has been done twice for drink-driving because he wouldn't allow himself to be driven by a woman, most especially not by his wife. And on one of these occasions she was pregnant, and responsible, and hadn't been drinking at all. On the other, she'd simply been responsible and confined herself to one glass of wine. This cut no ice with Supermike, who was out to show the Old Bill that not only could he hold his liquor like a man, he could drive like a berk.

Me? I have been blessed (thank you, Lord) with a wife who gets carsick if she doesn't drive. Yup, really. This means that we divide our travel tasks evenly between us. She does the driving and I do the drinking, and, on any journey exceeding ten minutes, she does the driving and I do the sleeping, slumped, open-mouthed and snoring, against the passenger door. Seems fair enough to me, and on the rare occasions that it occurs to me that MAYBE she doesn't get carsick at all, MAYBE she just holds an extremely low opinion of my driving, drunk or sober, I don't mind in the least. More of the testosterone bypass, I guess. Macho Mike thinks if you let a woman drive, or carve, you've lost the sex war. I think he's silly.

CHAPTER EIGHTEEN

Sex and Swopping

'Don't knock masturbation, it's sex with someone you love.'

WOODY ALLEN

THERE IS SOMETHING ABOUT HOUSEWORMERY, OR middle age, or me, or all three, that transfers sexual enthusiasm from the late-evening to the early-morning slot.

This is actually the most successful form of contraception yet devised, since no household containing two children under eight, five cats and a dog with a bladder condition will permit any rumpy-pumpy to be indulged in between the first and second cups of early-morning tea.

The solution that suggests itself, namely to wake self and spouse up a whole lot earlier, would be all very well for those whose five-year-old daughter does not transfer herself from her bed to theirs every night at any time between being carried in the other direction at adults' bed-time, and dawn.

She has completed one whole night in her own bed in five years, ten months and one day. But who's counting?

Furthermore, her preferred, nay enforced, territory is the centre of our admittedly large bed, separating the two of us by the simple expedient of sleeping with her head on that shoulder of her mother not occupied by a cat, and with her feet in my crutch. Quite often she kicks, and not only is she accurate, but I'm sceptical that she's doing it in her sleep. This means I have to sleep facing away from her, and while my back is turned the pair of them nick the duvet.

Not only the daughter, but at least three strategically placed cats form a prophylactic barricade that would easily repel a more ardent and less exhausted Houseworm than I am.

The cats choose her side of the bed ever since they chose mine and I taught them to fly.

(What? Oh, you just bring your knees up to your chest, hold the bedclothes tightly under your chin, and straighten your legs out as violently as possible. It's all to do with vectors, I think.)

SO WHAT'S TO DO, BIG BOY?

It is a fact generally acknowledged that if Dad is taking the children to school, his spouse can settle in front of GMTV or *The Times* without bothering about make-up, and drink her coffee in peace. The corollary of this theorem is that if SHE is taking the children to school an extra twenty minutes has to be slotted into the schedule in order to allow her to don the full street slap, together with matching shoes and handbag, or designer jeans at least.

For whose benefit, you may well ask, is this preening undergone? Any male reader can here and now disabuse himself of any idea that might be flattering his male ego with the notion that all this unnecessary titivating is for the benefit of the opposite sex, namely him.

What it is, is part of the school-gate one-upwomanship (or at least the avoidance of the one-downwomanship that turning up in no make-up and wellies would engender), NOT a signal of womanly attractiveness and availability, no matter what the boors in the saloon bar may imagine; and Houseworms hoping for a bit of inter-parental intercourse can forget it.

Quite right, too. There's nothing like falling in love with your daughter's best friend's mother (or father, for that matter) for initiating serious disharmony outside the school gates, all around the housing estate and throughout the Carol Service.

On top of which (or whom), those who think this sort of peccadillo can be kept secret, or even quiet, clearly have no experience of the broadcasting facilities of the PTA.

We school-gate derelicts don't even have jobs to distract us from close observation of every move our fellows make, and inter-parental jiggery-pokery makes a much more interesting alternative to the afternoon soaps, where not even the accents, let alone the acting, resemble real life.

There are three options open to the horny Houseworm, and only one of them works.

The first is a bit of the above, but he will rapidly discover that mothers in the process of delivering their children to school are not fantasizing about how they'd like to have Tracy's dad home for coffee prior to covering him in baby oil and rogering him senseless until they both have to get dressed to pick the kids up.

Or if they do, none of them is likely to either a) admit it or b) act upon it.

This sort of true confession can generally be found among the letters pages of *Forum*, written by men who sign themselves 'Rowena of Essex, 28 and 36B'.

Men (and we do, we do) may think about sex every thirty seconds, but wives and mothers (and eventually Houseworms, as well) know that there isn't the time, or energy, or any hope of avoiding the PTA grapevine, and so seek solace elsewhere, where most, but not all, of the previously listed drawbacks apply equally.

I have never, until last week, been able to understand the sexual exploits, or the thought processes, or the stamina of old Ralph Halpern, or Mellor, or Peter Hall – getting through four marriages and sharing the ups and downs (and ins and outs) with the readers of the *Daily Mail* – or ANY of these high-powered guys with demanding jobs, established marriages, several children, and brains stored neatly in the ends of their dicks.

Now it has been explained to me.

The reason they are successful and adulterous, and I am a Houseworm with a fidelity problem, is that their lives run on pure testosterone, and mine ran out years ago. The big T is what makes your average achiever first ambitious, then successful, then (or therefore) attractive and frequently divorced. Their ambition deprives them of the usual youthful sexual rites of passage because they are too busy with their careers. Their careers in turn provide them with the success that means they are attractive to women and have lots of opportunities for matinée nookie, and their high profiles provide them with the *News of the World* team which tends to ensure that Mrs High-flier gets to hear all about it and takes them to the Divorce Court for a mega-bundle.

This means, I'm afraid, that the boys in the saloon bar are right. There is something wrong with me. If I was any sort of a real man, I'd be out there heading up my restaurant empire at all hours of the day and night and sweeping female staff and customers off their feet and into the broom cupboard at every opportunity.

What better profession could there be for unlimited nookie? You meet lots of stunning women, you get to employ stunning waitresses, and you don't need any excuses for coming home shagged out at three in the morning. So why am I at home all the time folding the laundry? Partly too old, of course; partly too ugly (or I thought so until I read about D. Mellor); partly too enthusiastic about the charms of the breadwinner, and yup, the testosterone bypass.

Seems to me testosterone can't be all good, though. I mean look at David Mellor; I know it's not easy, but try.

Here is a bloke who says he's happily married. His colleagues say he's really seriously clever and definitely in the fast lane, and his success has ensured that women are attracted to him in spite of some pretty serious drawbacks of a more obvious nature. But good old testosterone does for him in no time at all. All his powers of analysis, all his perception and intuition, all his knowledge of the historical evidence and the future probabilities of his given course of action are entirely submerged in testosterone and he follows the member's member into Ms de Sancha, ridicule and a lucrative line in political commentary. I mean this guy was supposed to be CLEVER!

Anyway, the testosterone route to sexual nirvana and marital oblivion is clearly a non-starter for the Houseworm. The Houseworm does think about sex a lot, or at least as much as any executive of the same age with a secretary or two. But Mr Businessman, poor sap, thinks his attempts to woo Ms Blonde Balloobas from Tele-sales into a mucky weekend at some tax-deductible conference will be a) successful, b) a secret from the typing pool and c) NOT the cause of the shrieks of laughter that seem to stop suddenly every time he comes back from lunch early.

The Houseworm, on the other hand, is fully aware that Mrs Blonde Balloobas, wife of Mr Balloobas who travels a lot (in leather goods) and tells him man-to-man stories about Nigerian air hostesses and Thai hookers, is a lot more valuable as someone who can collect his children from school at a moment's notice and hang on to them until he can persuade the car to start, than she is as a proposition for morning coffee and a ham-handed pass that will, whether reciprocated or not, lead inevitably to much merriment at the school gates and the loss of a mutually supportive childcare system.

The Houseworm is similarly limited in his opportunities for other carryings-on AWAY from the school gates. This is, as British Rail would say, 'due to operational difficulties'. That is, when the executive with the pure gristle brain finds himself into an afternoon of houghmagandie at the Biggleswade Hilton, he need only call home to say he's been tied up (if that's his thing) and will be back late.

The Houseworm has two children to collect at three o'clock and, short of imposing an unusually large number of car break-downs on that nice Mrs Balloobas, there's no way he can get out of it. The thing about adultery is that it DEPENDS on there being some long-suffering spouse, sitting by the matrimonial fire and dealing with such items of real life as child-collection, supper and measles, thus freeing the testosterone-driven executive to rivet his secretary whenever she, and his schedule, permit.

THAT'S why the domestic spouses get so CROSS!

Infidelity is one thing, but using the injured party as an aid to availability is another.

This finally brings us to the third alternative, namely conjugal fidelity and/or self-abuse. Why this last should be thus referred to is a mystery to me, and all those at the back shouting 'we always knew you were a wanker' can siddown and shuddup until such time as they can demonstrate that they aren't.

Portnoy's complaint is no more a complaint than self-abuse is abusive of the self, but let that pass.

The advantages of solo sexual fantasies over the beast with two backs formed by Mr Executive and someone who looked a whole lot better in the hotel bar the night before than she does on his pillow at 8 a.m., are so numerous and obvious that some might consider them not worth listing, but for the benefit of the likes of Messrs Mellor, Hall, Pantsdown et al., I shall try.

— Fantasy sex objects (FSOs) do not watch you weaving your way across a night-club dance floor through three hundred people all of whom are under twenty-five, and then reject your advances thus: 'Fuck off, Grandad!'

– FSOs do not giggle with their friends beforehand, and tell them all about it afterwards, giggling even louder.

– FSOs look EVEN BETTER with their clothes off.

– FSOs do not report you to your organization's politically correct Wimmin's Officer for sexual harassment.

– FSOs do WHATEVER YOU WANT THEM TO!

– FSOs do not turn out, once in your bed, to have zits, bad breath or the curse.

– FSOs are NEVER HIV positive or have Aids or the clap.

– FSOs do not have children who wake up wanting a glass of water, or pets that wake up and want to join in.

– FSOs do not decide at 8 a.m. that YOU looked a lot better in the bar the night before and start screaming the place down.

– FSOs do not make accusations of rape before, during or after; not even a long time after, when their psychotherapist TELLS them they've been raped.

– FSOs do not want you to get rid of your wife and children so that they can marry you.

– FSOs do not get pregnant.

– FSOs do not even *want* to have your baby.

– FSOs do not sell your story to the *News of the Screws*, with full-colour pictures.

– FSOs do not want to be told that you love them from your sitting-room telephone on Christmas Eve.

– FSOs are not jealous that you have a real sex life as well.

– When you go on holiday with your family, FSOs do not break into your home and boil your daughter's pet rabbit.

It has long been a maxim among the more laddish men of my acquaintance that it is a serious mistake to bed anyone who has less to lose than you do. This must have come as news to D. Mellor, or else he did know, but he forgot. It has always seemed to this particular testosterone-free zone, that risking all for sex is a mug's game, but then I suppose I could be persuaded that what these poor saps were was lonely. If so, why wait to get caught before dumping, or being dumped by, the spouse?

Nearly all divorces seem to spring from a bit of the other, and bad marriages from staying together for the sake of the children (or his career).

Housewormery is clearly the answer to marital risk. He's too tired for all that malarkey, and if she's at it, he'll be too tired to notice.

Mind you, she may go off because of the boredom (SWFC syndrome) of being married to someone more interested in getting the children to bed than his leg over. This exercise in bemusement is going to end up being referred to as HWCW syndrome, or Houseworms Can't Win.

Twenty-four years and four children later we're still together, and the wife is married to a Houseworm with a self-generated reputation for being a kept man, a whoopsy, a wanker AND faithful to his wife.

I'm going to look an awful damn fool when the male menopause strikes and I'm sued for divorce on the grounds of adultery with somebody I met at a publishing party.

Still, as the bloke said as he fell past the twelfth floor of the skyscraper, so far so good.

Luck? Sure. But as Arnold Palmer once pointed out, the more he practises the luckier he gets.

My saloon bar *compadres*, I am informed by a tame psychologist, feel uneasy around women and therefore want to spend as much time as possible with other blokes.

Brought up as I was in South Africa, where these sorts of unhealthy predilections have long been part of the social whirl, I guess I must have reacted against it.

I had a gay actor friend who was once 'got at' by about thirty rugger-buggers in a bar.

Finally, after the usual round of 'backs against the wall' and other limp-wristed jokes, he became slightly hysterical and said that if he'd known that rugby involved a great deal of close physical contact with large sweaty men, at the end of which everyone took all their clothes off and jumped in a bath together, he'd have signed up years ago.

Needless to say, they beat him up.

Can I get this published under a pseudonym?

CHAPTER NINETEEN

Summer Daze

'Summer is icumen in, lude sing Cucku'

ANON

'CUCKU', IS ABOUT RIGHT, TOO. THERE IS NOTHING on earth better suited to bring home to the average (oh, all right then, *below*-average) Houseworm the facts about men, women, children and domesticity than the long (try interminable) summer holidays.

This, for those of you who don't know (why, hello there, boys), is the period centred around August when all those expensive schools send your children home so the teachers get a well-earned rest, your working partner, plumb tuckered out by all that client entertaining through June and July (Wimbledon, the Test Match, Royal Ascot), spends the evenings out on the lawn with a glass in their hand wondering aloud whether the herbaceous border couldn't do with watering, and you, the dumb Houseworm that you are, have to get up an hour earlier and go to bed an hour later just to keep up with the extra cooking and the laundry. Then, of course, there are OUTINGS, TREATS and, worst of all, THE SUMMER HOLIDAY.

We'll start with outings, just so you can get the idea from the point of view of the poor bloody infantry. It is a common occurrence among the domestic classes that one individual speaks as follows to another: 'Are you taking the kids out at all these holidays? If so, why don't we do it all together . . . it'll be much easier!'

It should be written in letters of fire on the foreheads of Houseworms that a problem shared is not a problem halved, it is a problem compounded, and that an outing is NOT improved by turning it into a joint venture. What on earth makes you think that exposure to your own children for up to twelve hours a day will be IMPROVED by simultaneous exposure to other people's?

After three days of 'WHEN WE WERE AT SCHOOL YOU SAID WE COULD GO ON AN OUTING IN THE HOLIDAYS', we went on a picnic with our ex-good friends Tony and Sue, their two children and three of ours. Our highly intelligent eldest wisely claimed a subsequent engagement and remained wrapped in bedclothes, Nirvana and, for all I know, Acapulco Gold. I wish I'd joined him.

There is only so much jolly *bonhomie* this Houseworm can enjoy with a man who demonstrates his assertiveness training by constantly telling anyone who will listen that his wife is all but half-witted (haha) because of having nothing to do all day while he is out earning a living, and as for me, if I had a proper job he might stop referring to me and his wife collectively (haha) as 'the girls'. Any instructions about shutting up are generally attributed to (haha) 'the wrong time of the month, eh?'.

The revelation is the extent to which the wife and children connive at their Lord and Master's little joke. They giggle affectionately and Sue makes sure he gets the sort of beer he likes, the last slice of smoked salmon, and peels his bloody quails eggs for him. Throughout all this he sneers a lot and points out repeatedly that it's just as well he and Penny have jobs or else (haha) who would PAY for all this, eh?

Meanwhile, their eldest son (12), egged on by his role-model hero, has demonstrated his recently learned judo on Rosie (5), who is now in floods and wants to go home and frankly I'm with her. Our number-two son has gone off for a walk by himself and Joe and their youngest are taking turns demanding arbitration from their respective parents in the matter of who did what to whom. The fact is, that if you ever hear a parent whose method of dealing with this is to say 'I don't want to hear about it . . . you kids sort it out!', you can guarantee that you are listening to the father of the aggressor. Do NOT go ANYWHERE with this sort of person. Do not have them in your home, and install automatic-fire machine-gun nests around your property to deter anything resembling a spontaneous visit. Do not be misled by the charm, wit, intelligence and beauty of his wife into thinking he must have some redeeming feature. She, in fact, is it; but after twenty years of being told she's useless, she now believes that she can't live without him and that he represents all that's positive about the male hero.

Sorry, Germaine, you were right all along.

Do you realize that while you were on this picnic the lawn grew half an inch? When you get home there'll be work to do.

Think how much the lawn can grow in two weeks. Most people spend most of their lives acquiring surroundings that they find comfortable, beds they like to sleep in, and people amongst whom they feel safe and secure and content. Then once a year, at enormous cost and frequently using money that they have borrowed, they leave these surroundings in order to subject themselves to the tedium of travel involving noisy, uncomfortable and often dangerous machinery designed to transport them hundreds or thousands of miles to surroundings of which they have no prior knowledge, to sleep in beds they are not at ease with, and live among people they neither know nor care to know.

This is called the family holiday, and when (if?) they get back at the end of it their lawn will resemble Equatorial rain forest, their courgettes will win prizes as marrows, and everything else will have gone to seed. In the house the burglar alarm will have been set off hourly until the police were forced to break in and silence it, the cat which set it off will be on the point of death by starvation, locked, as it has been for a fortnight, in the spare bedroom, and the boarding-kennel will have ensured that their springer spaniel is returned to them having contracted both enteritis and hardpaw. Their sixteen-year-old daughter will be pregnant by a Spanish waiter, and their nineteen-year-old son will still be out in Spain facing three years in prison after falling in with a crowd of English football supporters who encouraged him to urinate in through the open window of a passing police car.

We went to Wales. Weeeellll, UT has a cottage there, OK?

WE went on OUR OWN!

Imagine, if you will, a remote, white Welsh cottage which sleeps, comfortably, two adults, two dwarves and a chihuahua, becoming home for two weeks to four adults, two large children and a Great Dane with a flatulence problem. The second son implored us never to reveal to any of his schoolfriends where this holiday took place, since the mockery of those who generally spend two weeks in Rock, Cornwall, getting stoned with their West London mates, followed by another four in St Lucia or Goa, was getting to be more than the lad could bear.

'Not to worry,' commanded the Househead. 'We'll go for great walks and visit The Rare Breeds Centre.'

After her family, who needs rare breeds?

What is it about Wales? Whenever you are crying out for someone to torch a cottage, there's not a Welsh Nationalist in sight, and the Welsh hills are entirely inhabited by relicts of the Sixties, still wearing kaftans and doing leatherwork and making organic goats' cheese. And it rains. Boy, does it rain. And guess what . . . this cottage has been carpeted to UT's specification; and while he may like the idea of the spartan life, in reality his tastes and inclinations run more to pale beige shag-pile right up to the front door, and even the kitchen has carpet tiles for God's sake. Or maybe that's Evie.

The result of these arrangements is that supervising the donning and removal of wellington boots at every exit and entrance, and the carpet cleaning occasioned by the children who got by me, and the fact the dog doesn't HAVE any wellington bloody boots, becomes something of a full-time job.

Did I mention that at the last minute the breadwinner and soul mate undertook to do a 5,000-word article for one of the colour sups? 'How could I get out of it?' she demanded. 'And anyway we need the money so that we can go somewhere else next year, right?' No-one could ever accuse this Houseworm of not being able to tell which side his bread's buttered once it has been forcefully applied to his forehead.

So naturally, the laptop clicks merrily away alongside the solid fuel Rayburn that provides the only warmth in the house, if you don't count the open fire, and I don't. The open fire has a chimney that draws successfully only when there is no wind. The slightest gust from any direction causes a down draught which fills the cottage with smoke, and momentarily obliterates all memory of how horrid it is outside in an overwhelming desire to escape. This travesty of the heart and focus of a country cottage is supposed to consume logs, so aided only by those children forcibly ejected from their beds with much wailing and gnashing of teeth, or those still small enough to be misled into thinking they are enjoying themselves, the Houseworm gets in logs from the log store, the construction of whose roof was personally supervised by Dafyd ap Griffith in about AD

604 and which has leaked spectacularly ever since, with the result that down draught or not, the soggy lumps of hawthorn, elder and holly are too wet to burn anyway.

Coal, on the other hand, is required for the Rayburn (q.v.), and this is kept, again, in a store that can only be reached from outside and round the back, see . . . the exercise will do you good, bach. See if it doesn't!

It doesn't. More especially since if you keep your coal store full for your own visit, and constantly topped up, as UT does, and you use the big lumps on top because they are easy and cleaner to handle, then by the time the houseworm-in-law or whatever I am arrives ('There'll be plenty of coal, boy, so you don't need to bother your 'ead, see!'), what you have is a coal store full of black dust, which may, or possibly may not, conceal whole lumps within it but there's only one way to find out, see?

Coal dust is even less easy to remove from shag-pile than mud. Also, it is an immutable physical law that no appliance designed to burn solid fuel (logs, coal, straw, children) has a capacity sufficiently large to keep it going through the night. By 6 a.m. (REGARDLESS OF THE TIME WE BANKED IT UP!) the chill is sufficient, even in summer, to have me shovelling soggy coal in my dressing-gown and wellies in the hope that by 8 a.m. the stove might be persuaded to produce the necessary hot water for the cup of tea which, should I be deprived of it, may finally push me over the edge. It is to wives who are going through this sort of experience, that men like Tony say, 'What's up? Change of life, is it? God, is that what's for lunch? See you when we get back from the pub, OK?'

Speaking of pubs, we found one in Wales (OK, it MIGHT have been the only one) whose landlord, when asked if we might eat in the pub with our children, said, 'In the car outside, or on a leash . . . that's the rule around here,' so we left.

A Welsh joke: Small, sad, single Englishman on holiday in Wales is looking miserably into his drink in the corner of a valley pub, when the landlord asks him what's the matter. 'I'm lonely,' he says. 'All the Welsh people I meet are unfriendly as soon as they hear my English accent, and I like Wales and would like to get to know the people.'

'It's history, that is,' says the landlord. 'The English have been rude to the Welsh for so long that nobody trusts an Englishman straight away. But if you make a bit of an effort, see, you'll find us very forgiving. Try and learn a bit of Welsh, just to show willing, and see if you don't make a friend!'

Next day, our hero, having learnt that the Welsh for 'Good-day' is 'Bore da' or something that sounds like it, steps out into the village street, and as an extremely old local, all tweeds and whiskers, wobbles towards him on his bicycle, he shouts out a cheery 'Bore da!' The response is immediate: 'Get out of the road, you stupid Welsh git!'

Back to our jolly fun-filled family fortnight. There is only so much walking in the pouring rain that can be undertaken by six people and a dog before the cottage begins to resemble (and smell like) an Oxfam clothing warehouse in an Equatorial rain forest. With the Rayburn fired up to max in a vain attempt to dry soaking clobber, most items can soon be seen to sport an interesting mould, which necessitates, for the Houseworm, extended use of an unfamiliar and even more truculent washing-machine than his own. Tumble-dryer? HA! 'The only dryer you need, boy, is the Good Lord's wind, see!' (I let the possibilities of this remark of UT's go by for the sake of religious harmony.)

The result of all this is that by day four, or possibly five, we are in familial confrontation mode, which is like an industrial dispute but with dirtier tricks. On the one side the Househead is extolling the virtues, between laptop taps and cups of tea, of continued bracing walks in the wonderful fresh air, and don't be so silly a little rain never hurt anybody. The dog is clearly on her side. Ranged against them, and forming the opposition shock troops, are Joe and Rosie, in profound agreement for the first time in their lives. Walking is horrible, wet, cold and muddy. Their clothes are heavy, scratchy and smelly because Daddy still hasn't dried them, and the only nice thing about walking is when Daddy says we have to stop at a pub and we get crisps, but not even crisps at that pub where we can eat lunch in the dining-room is going to get either of them out of the house once more unless the sun comes out, so there.

The suicide squad duo's 'give me videos or give me death' heroics are supported in subtler (some would say more devious) ways by their elder siblings. Number One points out that there are only so many sheep, regardless of the individuality of colouring and horn-formation, that one undergraduate can take, and he got beyond that number on day two at The Rare Breeds Centre. If, he says, he wishes to see a sheep, he will look out of the window. He will not get in a car, even if he is allowed to drive, in order to travel 20 miles to see an identical animal but with funny horns. If we wish him to, he says, he will take the car, all three siblings and thirty quid and they'll all go to the movies and give the 'rents (that's us) time and space to get UT's cottage a bit more comfortable. Provided, that is, that he gets the thirty quid up front.

Number Two says that this sounds like fun, especially if we are talking thirty quid EACH, which we are not. BUT, he says, this is only a temporary solution to our ennui problem, and that he personally has no further desire to spend his evenings playing Monopoly with a set that is several items short of complete, or draughts or chess with, for the same reason, coke-bottle tops for pawns and kings, and there's that village Post Office where they've even got *Cliffhanger* for rent and what we need is a video player. (Here I can hear UT's voice saying, 'You don't want that stuff, boy. Television is bad enough, see, but that pornography rots the brains of the young!' I think UT believes a video recorder is something that plugs straight into Red Hot Dutch without benefit of a satellite.) We have, in fact, got the use of UT's telly, a blurry little item with a mind of its own and a UT-like determination to give you the Welsh-language programmes screened by S4C whether you want them or not.

BUT ... here the Houseworm, who has so far been keeping his head down, pulls out his ace of trumps. From beneath the sofa, where I had hidden it in the vain hope that it might not be needed, I produce our very own VCR, all the way from Surrey, and while a grinning Number Two tunes it in and *Pobol y Cwm* OUT, I hand over thirty quid and the car keys to the eldest along with instructions that if we see or hear any of them before supper-time they're dead meat. The Househead and I then take the dog for an exhausting walk up the nearest mountain, make soup for lunch, open a bottle of wine and retire to bed for the afternoon. Things began to look up, after that.

It will have become apparent to even the most cursory of readers that the functioning of the Houseworm depends to a large extent on the demon drink, a fact that I have absolutely no intention of denying. Life as a homebody is tough enough without depriving yourself of readily available anaesthesia. Were it not for such resources, I would long since have made the front page of every greasy tabloid through the simple expedient of having been discovered wearing nothing but an un-ironed Mondi blouse, cradling a chain-saw and giggling obscenely over the dismembered remains of several household appliances and a Great Dane.

Our earliest Celtic holiday (you know, the ones where the temperature seldom rises above chilly, the local idea of gastronomic bliss is a fish carry-out and a tin of mushy peas and where the reputedly spectacular scenery remains invisible behind a wall of mist and it chucks it down throughout) was one where we were going to enhance the health-giving properties of our outdoor loch-side sojourn by giving up the drink. By day four we'd had enough, and egged on by the threats of my wife and the imprecations of our six-month-old first-born, I made a round trip of some eighty miles just to get a bottle of Scotch. The provenance of this product is not a matter of chance, you know. If, in

Scotland's climate, whisky did not exist, it would be not only necessary, but essential, to invent it. The reason the Japanese can't synthesize the stuff, try as they might, is that their weather system, with its occasional sunshine, has not driven them to the desperate remedies daily demanded by the damp and chilly Scots.

Years ago I was lucky enough to work with Roy Dotrice, an actor of enormous talent and wit, who spent an entire morning describing a holiday he and his family had taken in the Caribbean. On this particular island, to hear Roy tell it, there was only one hotel (but that's not the best part), and every cottage had its own pool and its own bit of beach (but that's not the best part), and each cottage had a maid AND a butler (but that's not the best part), and every morning they scattered gold dust on the sands to make it sparkle, then they raked it (but that's not the best part), and the riding, water-skiing, sailing, scuba-diving and parascending were all supervised by qualified instructors and were free (but that's not the best part).

The best part was: YOUR CHILDREN GOT THEIR OWN COTTAGE! I was very young at the time, and didn't really appreciate the true cruelty of this bit of one-upmanship until I first clapped my bloodshot Houseworm's eye on UT's Welsh idyll. Holidays are generally pretty horrible, but if you take the children with you, you can make them REALLY unbearable. For the Houseworm, that is. The breadwinning types, revelling in their well-deserved time off from all that labour, can regard with amused concern the frustrations of a partner who has nothing to do all day throughout the year, simply having to do it more often for more people in less comfort and without the right equipment for two weeks in the rain.

Then you go home, and by God you've learnt to appreciate how lucky you are. Alerted by the fading of the homicidal look in your eye, the children, as soon as the breadwinner's got back in her box to polish the colour-sup piece that has provided her bolt-hole throughout the previous two weeks, start suggesting treats, like movies, trips to Brighton, OR HOW ABOUT BOTH?

Brainwashed by the pleasure of sleeping (when you can, between bouts of laundry) in your own bed, and blinking back the tears engendered by the sight of your own dear Thermomix, just where you left it, you agree.

By 10 a.m. on the day of this particular holiday treat, you have discovered that it rains in Brighton, too. Further, that Brighton offers restaurants, cinemas and car-parks, but not in anything like adjacent positions, and the wind and rain make travel between them less than yippee skip. Especially since Rosie has now remembered how last time she was in Brighton (the sunny day of 1992, this must have been) she went on a helter-skelter and NOWSHEWANTSTODOITAGAIN! Pointing out that it's raining gets me treated to an exact reproduction of my own voice, an octave higher, saying, 'Rain won't hurt you, you're waterproof!'

If you are in any doubt about the horrors of family treats involving trips to the seaside, try crossing the dual carriageway on the sea front of any large resort with the following: one tall, bespectacled undergraduate who is saving study time by walking and reading *Jude the Obscure* simultaneously; a 6 foot 2 schoolboy of A level age rendered deaf by being plugged by earphones into *Queen's Greatest Hits* at a volume that makes everyone NOT wearing the earphones think they're being attacked by a swarm of tin bees; an eight-year-old boy whose excitement at being out (so deprived is his homelife) leads him to demonstrate Teenage Mutant Ninja Turtle karate kicks within millimetres of any passing geriatric, and a large five-year-old who is pulling you along, with wails and imprecations, towards a helter-skelter that your superior height allows you to see is by no means open for business; its seventeen-year-old gum-chewing custodian, being possessed of a great deal more sense than you, reckoned, some hours since, 'Sod this for a game of soldiers', and went home.

Having negotiated the emotional minefield this discovery engenders in the daughter, having assuaged her grief with sweeties and gained the sanctuary of the local multi-plex, all that remains of the day out is to rediscover the fact that no sooner have you found your seats and had the second son empty a £3.50 tidal wave of popcorn round the ankles of everyone in your row, than the third son's bladder will get the better of him. He will require company. Once that's done, and just as the Ghostbusters are opening the haunted fridge that says GLAAAOOOOUUUUMMMM, or whatever it is, the daughter, too, will be caught short, and this is a very different matter. Me, I just walk her straight through the Gents to the sitting-down department and sit her down, fiercely ignoring her piercing enquiries as to why that man is standing like that and what's he looking at down there, since I reckon being a girlie makes her unlikely to appreciate the subtler aspects of the 'pee the fag-end down the drain before you run out of pressure' game.

What IS it about toilet or changing arrangements that make life for fathers of small girls, or, I am told, mothers of not-so-small boys, so incredibly difficult. At our local public swimming pool, if you are the mother (or simply the responsible female adult) in charge of small boys, and you have the sort of character that is typified by a loud upper-middle-class bray, then what you do is simply march into the Gents shouting instructions at your charges without deigning to explain or apologize for your intrusion to any of the stark-naked and extremely surprised men who thought they were momentarily safe from odious comparisons.

The reasons you can do this are firstly that as a woman in charge of children your rights take precedence over all others, and secondly that your sisters would not care to share their dressing facilities with gawping little boys, thunderstruck and giggling at the glories and variety of the female form unveiled. As for the men, well . . . none of them has got anything YOU haven't seen before!

Funnily enough, this solution, in reverse, is NOT open

to men in charge of young females. I can't for the life of me think why. So in motorway service areas, swimming-pools and cinemas the Houseworm, as the daughter gets older, will be reduced to hanging about outside the Ladies, in the hope that a perfect stranger will take pity on him and look after his daughter. I have offered the woman attached to the bray (*above*), my services for her male charges, but she was wise enough to know what sort of men offer to take little boys into lavatories, and declined, to the mortification of one gentleman whom she barged past while he was Johnson's Baby Powdering his parts.

The solution, if you can find one, lies in the discreet use of the Disabled Loo. So far we have never met, on our way out, someone in a wheelchair coming in. I pray God we never do.

And so, as summer sinks softly towards the mists of autumn, we leave the happy Houseworm as he packs his charges back off to school, and begins to contemplate the brief respite that has been granted him between the trials of summer and the true horrors that await him three months hence . . . at CHRISTMAS!

CHAPTER TWENTY

In Sickness and In Health

'Ivry sick man is a hero, if not to th' wurruld or aven to
th' fam'ly, at laste to himsilf.'

fiNLEY PETER DUNNE

THE ONSET OF WINTER MEANS THAT ONCE AGAIN WE CAN
indulge in the traditional activity of children going to school
in order to bring home every disease known to man and after
much personal suffering, hand them on to their family.

Women occasionally catch a cold. Men get flu.

It has, from time to time, been brought to my attention
that there are wives and mothers who think that their menfolk make an unnecessary fuss about their occasional illnesses
and that while a woman copes with a cold, two children,
the wrong time of the month and a hair appointment with

consummate skill and without recourse to either antibiotics or her bed, men start to whimper and retire upstairs at the first sign of a sneeze, and lie there requiring regular applications of hot toddies, soft-boiled eggs with soldiers and the complete silence of their offspring while they sleep between those moments when they can just about manage to focus on Sky Sport for which the telly must have been moved to the bedroom.

Since every woman I have ever met concurs with all the others in this jaundiced assessment of the suffering endured by their nearest and dearest, I feel duty-bound to set them right.

In the childbirth department, noble as we are, we are fully prepared to concede that the pain and discomfort suffered by our wives in the production of our children frequently exceeds the cramps, discomfort, tedium and pain induced by 'breathing along with her', or mopping a sweaty brow, or playing canasta between contractions, or having to go out for doner kebabs or doing our own washing-up, or putting up with constant phone calls from her mother that we men all endure within and without the delivery room.

BUT, to compensate for this, nature has ensured that in all other areas of suffering, balance is restored by the fact that men do not make more fuss in the face of indisposition, they actually suffer more. This is because they haven't gone through the baptism of fire that childbirth provides, after which any other form of suffering is a doddle.

For men, their natural sensitivity, uncalloused by the experience of childbirth (especially if they pass out at the sight of blood), combines with their innate depth of feeling to produce suffering on a scale undreamt of by the stronger sex.

I know, because I, too, have suffered.

Not a year goes by without this particular Houseworm feeling the familiar scratchy eyeballs, dry throat and pounding headache that presage a serious spell in bed accompanied by sympathetic visits from concerned loved ones and a great deal of TLC. Houseworms, however, have a problem. The Househead may very well be away, or simply loath to give up her breadwinning activities for a temporary career as a combination of Macmillan nurse, nanny, housekeeper, childminder, cook, masseuse, barlady and doctor. Also, maybe she doesn't give a toss.

This means that at the first sign of illness the Houseworm has to start laying out his stall so that adjustments can be made to mutually agreed responsibilities that finally result in him being able to take to his bed with tea, sympathy and a bottle of The Macallan.

This can often be a lot more difficult than it looks, but since three days in bed with a new John Irving novel, the TV and a temperature of 98.5 is as close as the Houseworm is going to get to a holiday this, or any, year, it is seriously worth the effort.

She's sitting tapping away at her laptop as I find (and then fold) the laundry while waiting for the supper to cook.

I have established that she has no commitments away from home for three days.

I pour her a drink.

I fold the laundry and wait, occasionally coughing quietly. 'Quietly' and 'weakly' can be synonymous. I find it takes longer than I would like for the feebleness of my condition to be noticed, but then she looks up and her eyes narrow with uxorial concern.

'Good God, haven't you got a drink?'

That's it. The clincher. She now KNOWS I'm terminal.

'Don't feel like it much, actually,' I say. Cough!

'You ill again?'

I'm not at all sure that I care for the 'again', but I breathe deeply and keep folding.

'Naah, 's'nothing, really. I'm fine.' Cough.

'C'mere,' she says, so she can feel my head.

'No, really. I'm fine. Let's eat.'

I open the Aga door and hang limply off the front rail, looking in.

'Come and let me feel your forehead!'

Now that said forehead has been warmed by careful insertion in the top oven, I comply, smiling weakly in a self-deprecating manner.

'Blimey,' she says as her cool hand clasps my brow. 'That oven's a lot hotter than usual. Is the supper OK?'

Rats.

'Told you I was OK,' I bluster bravely, and extract the supper and serve up.

'Isn't affecting your appetite, then?' she asks, as I help myself to what I consider to be a modest amount, sufficient to the needs of someone who houseworms.

'Trying to keep my strength up,' I mutter, and pour myself some vino.

This is not going quite as well as I had hoped.

By the following morning I really DO feel lousy, and wait for her to notice my shivering, quivering form when she gets back with the tea. Hell, it is her morning.

She looks down.

'You've got a cold,' she says. A cold? This has got to be pneumonia at least, and probably double. I wheeze 'I'm fine' at her and get up to pee.

When I get back she's holding out two tiny white pills that medical science will tell you contain nothing but sugar.

Oh God, it's homoeopathy time again, but since I figure I'll get at least three days of sympathy and concern before I allow myself to swallow the paracetamol and Scotch that will actually deal with the problem, I swallow this magic pixie-dust weakly and go back to sleep.

When I wake up I can hear the vacuum cleaner grinding away downstairs, and I remember that that was something I was really going to get around to sometime last week, and that if she's doing it now it's likely she'll notice that the dusting hasn't been done either, so I stagger weakly downstairs to say, 'Leave that. You get on with your piece for the *Standard*. I'll do it, later.'

She looks indulgent. 'Don't be a berk,' she says. 'I've done the *Standard* piece, and I enjoy doing this and you look like death. Go back to bed.'

I do, but sleep is out of the question. I can track her progress through the house as she does all the things I should have done in the housework department, and some of the things I did do, but not well enough. This is like some exquisite form of torture. I wanted a cop-out, and now I've got one I can't bear her showing me up, especially as she doesn't intend to at all. She really does like doing the stuff I find so mind-bogglingly tedious.

As long as she only does it occasionally.

I can remember when I quite enjoyed it on those terms as well. But even then I didn't get through it at the speed she is achieving as I languish in bed and worry about what else I've missed that she's about to come across.

None of this makes me feel any better.

The next thing I know she's standing over me with soup and saying, 'I'm going to get the children. Drink your soup while it's hot.'

Heh! AND there's golf from Augusta on telly this evening.

If more conclusive proof of male suffering were needed, which it ain't, how do you explain that the only time my wife has ever taken to her bed 'cos she felt grotty (childbirth excluded), was once with mastitis and once with Bjornholm's disease? And that's in twenty-three years. Now me, I get a migraine just about every week and to add to the laughs I'm allergic to quite a lot of shellfish. For twenty years it didn't stop me eating them, I just thought I kept getting bad ones.

After one particularly well-dressed crab, I was busily deciding at 3 a.m. which end of me to insert in the lavatory when she woke up and asked if I was being sick.

'If I'm not,' I quipped, 'I'll certainly do until someone who is comes along.' I found this so hilarious that I stopped reversing polarity and simply sat on the loo and threw up in the bath.

She wisely remained where she was until I'd hosed down the bathroom.

Eighteen years later we were in upstate New York with friends who insisted that if this was our first time in the States, which it was, we simply HAD to have 'little-neck clams and Maine lobster.'

Little-neck clams taste a lot better than they look, in that they look like buttered snot and taste of nothing at all. The Maine lobster was terrific, right up to the point where I informed our host of the number of times I'd been unlucky with crab and lobster and got a bad one. He didn't even look up.

He just said, 'Hell, that doesn't sound to me like getting bad shellfish. That sounds to me like an allergenic reaction!'

Penny says I turned pale green and the sweat broke out on my forehead instantaneously. By that time it was too late, and all we could do was await the inevitable.

The inevitable gave me until 2 a.m. before acquainting me intimately with the brand name of our hotel's sanitary equipment and a ceramic tile-pattern on the floor of the bathroom that I never wish to see again.

See? Men do suffer more than women, and the Houseworm is a particularly susceptible species in the suffering stakes.

I was talking to my friend the doc. He was among twenty or so people standing around in our sitting-room of a Sunday lunch-time, drinking our booze and making polite noises at each other. The reason for the gathering was the usual: namely, that I wanted someone apart from my immediate family to see what a great Houseworm I was, and that, contrary to expectations, I was not only thriving, but doing well enough to risk allowing outsiders to observe the phenomenon.

I have often been told that one of the early indications that I have taken on a few is that my voice and laughter volume tends to motor up towards the red line where it ceases to be bearable by those who are not actually hearing-impaired or aurally challenged.

What I was quietly asking the doc on this occasion was the

following: 'DOES EVERYONE FART MORE AS THEY
GET OLDER OR IS IT JUST ME?'

The total silence that greeted this perfectly reasonable
enquiry led me to believe that what I was holding could
possibly be my fourth, rather than my second drink.

The doctor looked at me with limited amusement.

'No,' he said, 'it's pretty universal. You ARE unique,
however, in being the only person who would bring the
subject up at a cocktail party.'

REALLY?

Doesn't anybody else MENTION this sort of thing?

I can't open a newspaper without being told a great deal
more about the sexual predilections of members of the Royal
family than I wish to know, but I DO find the Prince
of Wales' enthusiasm for becoming a tampon rivetingly
interesting. It's not my particular bag, but hell, different
strokes, right? I mean maybe if we all worked out what
everybody else was *really* thinking, we'd be more tolerant
and understanding and I wouldn't be stuck trying to find
out from their writing alone whether Germaine Greer and
Robert Bly are really Martians or just sound like it, or what
the average flatulence factor is in the forty- to fifty-year-old
male or whether peeing more or less or more slowly means
the onset of my prostate problem.

Yes, I *know* all men are hypochondriacs, but Houseworms
have little else to think about as they fold the laundry or
hoover the stairs. AHAH! THAT's why mothers are forever
forming gynae-groups at the school gates.

Gotcha.

But do you talk about it? The fact that male babies can
pee unerringly into your shoe while you're changing a
nappy or expel projectile vomit neatly over your shoulder
and all down the Househead's new Armani jacket, while
being burped, seem to me to be both interesting and
amusing, but you'd be astonished at the number of people
who don't think this sort of thing should be wheeled out
at dinner.

If you have one of those low-level, avocado-coloured bath-room suites, together with syphonic wotsis and side-by-side bidet, how many are allowed to make use of the facilities simultaneously? One friend, she of the Irish-Catholic upbringing, five children and subsequent life in a commune, once swore that in every house she ever lived in she was going to rip the loo out of the bathroom and install it separately elsewhere. She had had, she said, enough of her children coming in while she was luxuriating in the bath, and defecating loudly and noisomely 2 feet away.

She said it stopped her enjoying her glass of wine and Alice Thomas Ellis.

Nudity's another thing. My father-in-law, whom God preserve, was of a mind, when his children were young, that his wife should not be seen naked by her son lest it diminish his future awe at the miracle of the female form unveiled the first time he scored.

Decorum was further preserved, whenever his daughter intruded upon his bath-time ablutions, by recourse to a strategically floating flannel.

Fair enough, but taboos have moved on a bit. Haven't they? This house, first thing in the morning, resembles nothing more or less than a nudist colony, but does everyone's? Search me.

Problems only arise when it's not your nudity you find offensive, but other people's. The elder sons are now of an age when they bring home the odd (some are VERY odd) girlfriend or three. Now I don't mind them wandering about the landing in the altogether in the wee small hours should they feel the need, but I'm pretty damn sure that the sight of my *corpore collapso* waddling loo-wards might induce serious second thoughts about future bliss in the position of daughter-in-law. She can cover up modestly, as can, and does, our own dear eight-year-old son, whose views on nudity would have been applauded by John Knox, but the question remains, will I remember who's in the house when I need a pee at 4 a.m. and the youf are just stumbling in from a party and on their way to bed?

And whither they are bound, speaking of bed, is yet another of the Houseworm's areas of responsibility. Traditional mothers used to get the male breadwinner to 'have a little chat, man to man', with adolescent males while she handled the miracle of menstruation with the female offspring. Housewormery does not change this, and my only attempt at a 'man-to-man' chat resulted in number-one son saying 'Oh, puhleeeaaase' in a way that sort of left little to be said. But once grown-up children are at it anyway, is there any point in allocating visiting girlfriends the spare room only to be kept awake by the patter of late-night feet up and down the landing? Also suppressed giggles. And FINALLY, does the Houseworm, having been left a note about could he wake them at noon, take the sated pair a cup of tea in bed? I dunno.

Furthermore, *pace* JJ, no amount of exposure to familial nudity can dilute the interest of the testosterone-dominated male in the female form unclothed. We held a summer lunch party a couple of years ago, to which a leading publisher was invited together with his wife. He turned up with his mistress instead, a trophy model of about twenty-six with the sort of shape that makes Elle 'The Body' McPherson seriously consider a career in needlework.

After I had fed this tribe of the chattering classes, and had my moan about the buggers being too busy ruining each other's reputations with professional gossip to notice the wonderful food I'd spent three days preparing, or the exquisite state of the rose-garden, or anything except the breadwinner's sales figures, we all dispersed for tennis, swimming or whatever. At this point, the mistress simply took all her clothes off and dived into the pool. The memory still takes my breath away, and I have not as yet been forgiven by the four male tennis players, including sons one and two, for not whistling them up to share this vision of beauty, but that would have been *really* uncool, right?

I think she must have picked up some sort of echo from the surroundings. The previous owner of the house was what he called a committed naturist and his wife called a dirty old man. Men arriving to mow his lawns or deliver the diesel would report finding him scything nettles in the far field wearing nothing except a pair of cricket pads, from which we can deduce the precise height of the nettles.

When we lived across the green, he was always inviting us, but mostly while he looked at Penny, over for a swim. 1976, this was, and HOT.

When we arrived this seventy-six-year-old would be lying, bollock naked and brown as a nut, in the sunniest shelter of the swimming-pool area (an area ever since referred to as the 'Snake Pit') with a sun-bed already available next to him for the use of my bikini-clad wife.

'Oooh, take that off, it'll only get wet when you swim' was his opening gambit, but her natural modesty prevailed.

This scenario was re-enacted every weekend until one Saturday afternoon she turned up wearing a bikini whose microscopic areas of material were linked by three large brass rings. An evil glint came into the old bugger's eye and he went and turned on the sauna.

He didn't even try and get her to take her clobber off, he just said, 'Like to try a sauna? I'm having one.'

Like a lamb to the slaughter my wife said politely that she'd love to, and having had a swim, she and Hugh headed off into the 100-degree heat, he as naked as usual, and she clad still in her bikini.

Have you any idea what happens to brass rings in a temperature of 100 degrees centigrade? Yup. She was out of her bikini so fast old Hugh thought all his birthdays had come at once.

'Look,' he said, 'you're sweating already,' as he brushed a droplet off her left breast in a friendly fashion.

After that she gave him best and thought to hell with it.

Houseworms have more problems with taboos than housewives. They may be doing a real person's job, but they're still sex-obsessed male chauvinist pigs at heart, and don't you believe anything anyone else tells you.

CHAPTER TWENTY-ONE

A Houseworm's Handbook

'Bad cooks – and the utter lack of reason in the kitchen –
have delayed human development longest and impaired
it most.'

NIETZSCHE

THOSE WHO HAVE BECOME CONVINCED, LIKE ME, THAT
the future of world peace, the brotherhood of man and the
survival of the family are all bound up in the performance of
household tasks by those whose previous areas of expertise
were the club and the pub, need to know how to be a
Houseworm and survive.

The secret is not to try to be a mother, you haven't a hope,
believe me. The best you're going to do is fake it, and faking
it is what she's had more practice at than you, right? Or don't
you remember?

This is how it's done (please note that Ms Conran's two *Superwoman* books are twenty times the length of this chapter and will set you back more than this whole book. You do not want to be 'Superwoman'. What you want is time off.):

AREAS OF EXPERTISE

The Kitchen

It's painful, I know, but this is where you will spend most of your time, especially if it's also the room where everyone sits around gabbing, doing homework and saying, 'YUK, WHAT'S THAT?'

It therefore needs to be clean. Sort of. You can console yourself with the thought that if you have to clean up and tidy the kitchen every day, your nearest and dearest probably haven't had time to foul the sitting-room, so you can keep it as a parental retreat and clean it once a week.

Things without which the Houseworm cannot manage are:
  Washing-machine
  Cooker
  Fridge
  Freezer
  Microwave
  Vacuum Cleaner
  Ironing-board (to be used under duress only)
  Iron

Those without which he might manage, but not very well, are:
  Tumble-dryer
  Food Mixer or (preferably) Processor or (best of all) both
  Dishwasher

Those luxuries without which he will manage but not maximize the desired time off, are:

> Hand-held liquidizer for smoothing soups in the saucepan without having to wash the Processor as well
>
> Thermomix
>
> Gelatochef (This VERY expensive gadget will turn old bolts, nuts and engine oil into Model T Ford Ice-cream. Save up for one and your children will care for you in your dotage. It does not save you money over buying Häagen Dazs, but by God it uses up overripe bananas pretty creatively)
>
> Toasted Sandwich maker
>
> Aga

I know this last is only another form of cooker, but those who think so haven't had one and those who have never go without one again. You can even enrol on a COURSE about the things.

It also helps the Houseworm understand and appreciate the novels of Joanna Trollope, Mary Wesley and Alice Thomas Ellis.

Those things that he can manage very well indeed without are:

> Floor Polisher
>
> Any gadget advertised in the colour supplements as 'A kitchen revolution'

In the kitchen you will read the paper, clear up, drink coffee, clear up, chastise your offspring, clear up, supervise homework, clear up and suffer the inevitable nervous breakdown unless you fend it off daily with the contents of the wine bottle concealed in the tea-towel drawer.

But most of all you will cook.

The following is a three-week menu schedule that means you will never have to think about what to give them again.

MENUS *3 WEEKS = 21 DAYS

This is not a cookbook. It's meant to make the Houseworm's lot a little easier.

It's assumed that:

a) you have a recipe book.

b) you can read.

c) you do NOT think that carefully tried-and-tested recipes can be improved by the addition of whatever you just happen to have in the fridge.

d) you are not an enthusiast for what my mother insists on calling 'a little sloodge-up' and which consists of EVERYTHING she happens to have in the fridge.

e) you are aware that if the addition of a tablespoon of brandy is reputed to be a good thing, it does not follow that six tablespoons will increase the goodness proportionately. They won't. Sorry, Evie.

If you do not have a recipe book, I can recommend several by someone called Prue Leith, or failing that buy ANY Delia Smith book. Her recipes have the advantage of being simple enough for even the most half-witted Houseworm, with the added bonus that they actually work, and the final dish comes out exactly as described. This is not necessarily true of the *oeuvre* of the great Michelin three-star chefs, some of whom assume, God knows why, that you can recognize a bouquet garni at 300 yards in a bad light, whereas we all know you can't even spell it.

In general:

a) Never make stock. The supermarkets have stock concentrates in jars, cubes and powders (choose the jars) that are probably better than anything you could whip up from assorted bones and potato peelings and are a lot less likely to kill you off than the average domestic stockpot.

b) Bread should be as high-fibre and expensive as possible, even to the point of REALLY lashing out and making it yourself. That way it's got more nourishing ingredients than air, water and E numbers got up to look and taste like cotton wool.

Until I found a bakery that makes amazing malted granary bread (the one with whole grains in the flour) I used to make bread and freeze it weekly. That is, if I couldn't get the wife to do it.

She's better at it than me, all right? This is called delegation.

In any case, buy it in bulk and freeze it. Nothing thaws as quickly and conveniently as bread.

There are also seriously wonderful breads on every supermarket shelf these days, so buy baguettes and ciabattas and God knows what. (And what God knows is that those frozen semi-pre-baked rolls and baguettes sold by most supermarkets are a Houseworm's dream come true. They take about ten to fifteen minutes from frozen and make you look very cool indeed. They'll be better than anything you can do, and remember even Nico Ladenis draws the line at making his own bread.)

c) I have touched, elsewhere, upon staples (as in diet, not stationery) and happy the Houseworm who never runs out of:
    Bread
    Pasta
    Tinned Tomatoes
    Vegetable Stock Concentrate (the meat stocks won't do for everything, this will)
    Frozen Chicken Portions (thighs are best)
    Frozen Oven Chips (you do NOT want to get into deep frying, trust me)
    Onions

Potatoes
Butter or (if you MUST) yellow-coloured grease
Milk
Fruit Juice
Jam
Olive Oil (no sat. fat and tastes better than butter)
Flour (Wholemeal AND Plain)
Cheese
Eggs
Baked Beans
Frozen Peas
And, oh all right, Fish bloody Fingers
Your children's favourite cereal
Fresh Fruit
Salt and Pepper
Tea
Coffee
Grog

On these basics you can survive and your family thrive indefinitely, but it's also nice to have:

Garlic
Herbs
Spices
Dried Fruits
Rice
Pulses (tinned are quick and expensive, dried are cheap and laborious)
Biscuits
Treats (like Fray Bentos Steak-and-Kidney Pie in a tin)

For fresh meat and fish and fruit and veg, shop once a week and freeze whatever (meat or fish) won't keep until twenty-four hours before you need it.

Finally, NEVER SHOP WHEN YOU'RE HUNGRY!

Breakfast (if you insist)

All or any of the following:

Fruit Juice from the carton. (We have milk bottles on the breakfast table, too. Doesn't EVERYONE?)

Cereal. (Come on, even you can pour Crunchy Nut Corn-flakes.)

Porridge – winter only (instant rolled oats, preparation time 5 mins, instructions on the packet).

Toast, butter, etc.

Coffee (in a large enough jug to last you the morning).

Bacon and Eggs and Fried Bread and Tomatoes and Mush-rooms and Sausages should ONLY be attempted by enthu-siasts and only at weekends and only when there's no hope of lunch as well; and even then it's easier to take the family to the nearest transport caff and let THEM kill you.

AND TO FOLLOW:

Day One

Lunch: Minestrone Soup, Bread, Fruit/Cheese. NEVER make puddings for lunch!!

   (Tip: to break spaghetti into manageable chunks for soup, roll it all in a tea towel and crack it by running it over the edge of a table or worktop. Add a bit of chilli powder to *all* winter-type soups.)

Dinner: Leek-and-Fish Pie with Cheesy Pastry, Mashed Potatoes and Peas, Oranges in Caramel.

   (Tip: always add nutmeg (say ½ a teaspoon) to mashed potato, and the way to clean leeks is to peel off the outermost skin, trim but don't cut off the root end, sharpen the green end like a pencil and, holding it by the root end, push the tip of a knife into the leek so you can slice it lengthways to the green end. Turn it ninety degrees and do it again, then waggle the by now bushy end in a sink full of clean water. This way it all holds together.

Caramel is easiest and quickest if you ignore all those instructions about boiling sugared water. Simply melt sugar over a high heat, turning the pan so it runs about and doesn't burn, then, when it's brown enough (quite dark is best), *stand well back* and pour in boiling water.)

Day Two

Lunch: Hummus with Pitta Bread or Toast.

(Tip: if you've bought tinned chick-peas as I told you to, simply dump the drained tin contents (14 oz) into a processor bowl with two or three cloves of garlic, black pepper and lemon juice, then blend to a paste dribbling in good olive oil as you go. You'll end up with a smooth purée that gets *thicker* the more olive oil you add.)

Dinner: Spaghetti with Pesto, Salad, some bought-in Pud from Sarah Lee Inc.

Day Three

Lunch: Baked Potatoes filled with Grated Cheese.

Dinner: Lamb Chops, Mash* and Leeks*; Rice Pudding.
    * If you were a clever little Houseworm, you made too much mash and cooked too many leeks on Day One, so THAT's no bother. Ain't microwaves wonderful? They heat up cold coffee, too.)

Day Four

Lunch: Minestrone again (you did MAKE double quantities, didn't you?).

Dinner: Risotto, made with diced root veg and good stock and a few prawns (Quorn for veggies?), and Steamed Mange-touts; Cheese and Biscuits with Celery.

(Tip: I KNOW you're supposed to stand over risotto adding stock a tiny bit at a time to pre-fried Arborio rice, but to hell with it. Boil it, and chuck the other stuff in with some butter. We're after nutrition and spare time here, not a Michelin star.)

Day Five

Lunch: Bread and Cheese, Fresh Tomatoes and Chutney.

Dinner: Cod Fillets, Parsley Sauce, Boiled Spuds, Spinach; Fruit Compote (all those dried fruits I told you about are *very* low on time and trouble) and Custard (11 mins in Thermomix . . . NEVER buy that powdered muck. Custard is made with eggs).

Day Six

Lunch: Mozzarella and Tomato Salad, Hot French Bread Baguettes.

Dinner: Pasta Frittate, Tomato Sauce, French Beans; Bananas and Custard (remember the custard?).

(Tip: Pasta Frittate – start off with left-over spaghetti from Day Two – you ALWAYS do too much, remember?). Beat two eggs, grated cheese, chopped and fried onion if you like it, all together. Then add the spaghetti and mix it well before frying the whole thing in hot olive oil. Don't make this with pasta shells. Tomato sauce takes 5 minutes in the Thermomix. Make a lot, you're having tomato soup next week!)

Day Seven

Lunch: Roast Chicken, Roast Potatoes, Carrots and Beans; Bread and Butter Pudding.

(It's Sunday, OK? You have to make an effort! Baste the chicken with honey and mustard.)

Supper: Scrambled Eggs on Toast.

Day Eight

Lunch: Tomato Soup (tinned? Thinned down sauce?) with Garlic Croutons; Fruit and/or Cheese.

(Tip: make croutons in the oven, not by frying on top.)

Dinner: Mild Beef or Quorn Curry with Poppadoms and Rice; Fruit Salad (a virtuous way to use up the contents of the fruit bowl before the flies start writing you thank-you letters).

Day Nine

Lunch: Toasted Cheese Sandwiches.

(Tip: if you don't have a Toasted Sandwich Maker, make the sandwiches using squashy bread, like Mighty White, then pinch the edges together and shallow fry them to golden brown on both sides. Your children will love you and you will begin to look like Pavarotti. *See* 'leftovers and how to avoid them'.

Dinner: Sausages and Mash and Peas; Apple Crumble.

(Tip 1: try putting good olive oil instead of butter in the mash. Amazing. Tip 2: Crumble Mixture, made in a processor in the ratio 4 flour:2 fat:1 sugar, is the pastry-nerd's cop-out. Use the pulse button to mix it, and sprinkle sunflower seeds on the top before cooking. Tip 3: one of the best vegetarian recipes of all time is for Glamorgan sausages, viz.: take a double handful of sliced leeks (done in the processor) and a slightly smaller volume of grated cheese (from the processor), and the same of breadcrumbs (made in the processor) and salt and pepper and a pinch of mustard, and bind the whole thing together using a couple of eggs (save one egg-white and whisk it firm). Squidge the result into sausage shapes, roll them in the whipped egg-white and either fry them in shallow hot oil until brown on all sides, or freeze them separately on a sheet of cling-film on a tray. Once frozen, they can be tipped into a bag and they cook brilliantly from frozen.)

Day Ten

Lunch: Jacket Potatoes filled with Baked Beans and served with a Green Salad.

Dinner: Risotto (remember the curry?) with Shredded Chicken (remember Sunday Lunch?) and Sweetcorn (out of a tin!); Greek Yoghurt, Almonds and Honey.

Day Eleven

Lunch: Avocado Dip and Toast; Fruit.
   (Tip: it's just another dip, dude! Chuck a ripe avo into the processor with a clove of garlic and a dash of lemon juice and lots of black pepper. Whiz it and trickle in that nice olive oil until it looks like green mayonnaise. You don't know what mayonnaise looks like? Check out the supermarket, under 'Hellmans'.

Dinner: Shepherd's Pie and French Beans; Tinned Peaches and Cream.

Day Twelve

Lunch: Tomato Soup if there's enough left over, or open a tin.
   (On his birthday, my father was always allowed a tin of Heinz tomato soup, brought to the table hot, but still in the tin to prove that, just this once, no-one had buggered about with it.)
   (Tip: this time sprinkle lots of flat-leaved parsley (in winter) or basil (in summer) all over it,* and serve with those pre-baked, cook-from-frozen baguettes.)
   * If nothing else, herbs are what gardens are FOR!

Dinner: Fray Bentos Steak-and-Kidney Pie (straight out of the tin!), Boiled Spuds (lots!), Steamed Courgettes; Pears poached in Wine.

Day Thirteen

Lunch: It's Saturday . . . go out for pizza,

OR

Dinner: It's Saturday night, SEND out for pizza.
Either way, make omelettes for the other meal.

Day Fourteen

Lunch: Teriyaki Lamb (buy the marinade), Sauté Potatoes (remember the boiled spuds?), Broad Beans (Waitrose do 'em frozen); Banoffee Pie.

(OK, I'll tell you the recipes:

1) Get the butcher to bone a leg of lamb and flatten it out. Marinade (it means SOAK, OK?) the meat in teriyaki marinade for 24 hours, then roast it in a REALLY hot (250 degrees) oven for fifteen minutes, then keep it warm for 15 minutes and it will be perfect. No, it doesn't matter how big it is.

2) Banoffee Pie is the business for impressing diners of any age. Put two unopened cans of full-cream condensed milk in a saucepan, cover with water and boil for 3–4 hours with a lid on. If you leave the lid off and one of the tins has a weakness in the seal, you could end up covered in a mixture of boiling water and boiling toffee. When their time is up DO NOT OPEN THE TINS. Let 'em cool down first.

Meanwhile make a shallow pastry case with shortcrust pastry, or mix a packet of digestive biscuits and melted butter to a biscuit-crumb base in your processor and pack it into a loose-bottomed flan ring. Cook it a bit so it gets crunchy but not burnt. Take the two tins out just before lunch, open both ends and push the caramel toffee they now contain (magic, huh?) out onto your pastry or biscuit base. Smooth it out, top with sliced bananas (first) and creme fraiche (second), then grate some dark chocolate over the whole thing. You CAN use whipped double cream, but I think that's just gross, don't you?)

Supper: After Banoffee Pie, who needs supper? Oh, all right then, Cheese and Biscuits.

Day Fifteen

Lunch: Lamb and Lettuce Sandwiches; Fruit/Cheese.

Dinner: Eggs Florentine; more Sauté Spuds; Gooseberry Fool.

(Tip: the great thing about spinach is that it retains almost its own weight in butter, so beat in as much as your cholesterol level will allow and season with salt, pepper and nutmeg. Make the fool from frozen fruit and custard, or cream if you're rich. If you're THAT rich, what are you doing here?)

Day Sixteen

Lunch: Onion Soup like *Maman* used to make.

(Tip: brown sliced onions in butter and oil, add a good strong stock and top with a slice of bread covered in cheese. Grill before serving and be careful . . . onions and melted cheese are both hotter'n hell and, what's more, they stick to your chin.)

Dinner: Chicken *à la crème*, French Beans, Rice; Fruit Sorbet (or save up for a Gelatochef).

Day Seventeen

Lunch: *Charcuterie* and *Crudités* with Hot Bread and Aioli (Garlic Mayo).

(Tip: just about every supermarket now has a great deli counter where you may have to shell out more than you do for soup, but think of the time you're saving.)

Dinner: Macaroni Cheese, Green Bean and Almond Salad; Fruit Yoghurt.

Day Eighteen

Lunch: Fresh Tomato and Pasta Salad with Pesto Vinaigrette; Cheese/Fruit.

(Tip: stir a tablespoon of pesto, bought if you must, into ¼ pint of good oil and vinegar dressing.)

Dinner: Beef (or Quorn) Carbonade,* Mash, Peas; Treacle Tart.

* It's just a good stew made with Guinness or similar.

Day Nineteen

Lunch: Avgolemono with Garlic Focaccia Bread.

(It's easy. Egg, lemon and rice soup like we all thought was amazing in some filthy Greek taverna, and you can even BUY Focaccia Bread. But it's quick and easy to make and you can worry about the soup while it proves.)

Dinner: Fish and Chips (go on, lash out); Mars Bar Ice-cream.

Day Twenty

Lunch: Mushroom Quiche and Salad.

Dinner: Cheese Fondue; Fruit.

(Tip: Cheese Fondue is great for children, does not run the same risk as the boiling oil required for meat fondue, uses up all the stale bits of bread you've collected over three weeks, and your family have to serve themselves. It is rumoured that you mustn't drink red wine with it. Bollocks.)

Day Twenty-one

Lunch: Roast Beef, Brussels Sprouts, Carrots, Roast Potatoes; Steamed Apple and Mincemeat Pudding (Delia, who else?).

(Tip: buy rolled rib, or (cheaper) topside, and seal it in hot fat in a frying-pan before roasting. Roast potatoes go into soup for next week's potato-and-onion staple. If you liquidize it, the brown bits nearly vanish.)

Dinner: Nursery Food – Boiled Eggs, Soldiers; Fromage Frais with sugar on.

Follow these last with a tot of The Macallan and an early night, because tomorrow you start the whole three-week cycle again! No-one will ever notice you're repeating yourself tri-weekly (try weakly?) and for why? Firstly, because none of your nearest and dearest can remember what they got for lunch yesterday, let alone three weeks ago, and secondly, you have about as much chance of sticking to this schedule as you have of scoring with Mother Teresa.

Within five days, when she says, 'What's for lunch?' you will reply, 'Lunch? Oh, shit.'

Then you will both open a packet of peanuts, pour yourselves a drink, and get on with your lives.

Leftovers and How to Avoid Them

Finally, once you have done all that cooking and your children have said YUK, you will be faced with the 'waste not, want not' inclination to hoover up after them and eat the leftovers from children's supper. This is not a good plan. Oven chips and ketchup may not do a five-year-old much harm, but you already weigh fifteen stone *and* you've still got Macaroni Cheese to come, remember? The best advice ever given on the subject of leftovers is as follows:
1) Chuck 'em out;
OR
2) If you can't bear the waste, stick 'em in the fridge until they grow a furry overcoat, THEN chuck 'em out. You won't mind at all.

This advice does not apply to *planned* leftovers like pasta and rice and soup ingredients which are not leftovers at all, but the ingredients of lunch for the day after tomorrow. You were just ahead of the game, right?

CHAPTER TWENTY-TWO

Yule Do

'People can't concentrate properly on blowing other people to pieces properly if their minds are poisoned by thoughts suitable to the twenty-fifth of December.'

OGDEN NASH

IT WAS FOUR IN THE AFTERNOON OF CHRISTMAS EVE, at the end of The Major Year, and my sister was contemplating her enormous, but totally unadorned Christmas tree, and enough as yet unprepared grub to feed Sarajevo for a fortnight, when one of the many guests invited to spend the week with her asked if there wasn't something she ought to be getting on with, seeing as how time was rolling merrily along.

'I am waiting,' she said, 'for the slaves.'

The slaves, the while, were rolling less than merrily along the A34 in a line of traffic that stretched out to the crack of

doom. From the back seat the smalls were getting stuck into
their first Christmas carol:

> There's a PARTy in the DUNnee,
> Do you want to COME?
> Bring your OWN toilet PAPer,
> and YOUR BIG FAT BUM!!

Then they screamed with laughter and did it again. And
again.

I blame *Neighbours*.

When packing up the family for the biennial Christmas
gathering, the wily Houseworm will load up the Renault
Espace (the only production vehicle into which my family
will fit) with children, clothes, food and drink, dog, dog
food and drink, bicycles, Christmas presents and wife, and
then check himself into a health farm for the duration.

Should he not embark on this course of action, he will
rapidly rediscover the fact that the shortest measurable unit
of time is that between driving out of the gate and Rosie
asking if we're there yet. He will also find that the above list
of essentials do not actually fit, even into a Renault Espace,
and that it is at this point that the wife will valiantly offer to
take her dog, plus one big son to look after it, in her car.
This leaves the Houseworm with the two smalls, another son
whose Walkman ensures a communication level approaching
zero, and an 80-mile drive with a pair of handlebars sticking
in his ear.

He begins to hope that the dog gets carsick.

It is only after he has made three return trips to the house
to get Joe's coat, Rosie's wellies and the bag of bananas and
little cartons of juice designed to distract them both from
the tedium of the journey, that he sets out in pursuit of
the breadwinner who sailed blithely out of the drive fifteen
minutes earlier in an unencumbered cloud of serenity and
Classic FM.

The entire south-east of England, it rapidly becomes

apparent, has chosen this very minute to take to the road as well, and by the time we've reached the stationary triple line of traffic on the M25 fifteen miles away, Rosie has eaten four bananas and says she feels sick, Joe says he needs to pee NOW, and son number two has traded in his Walkman for U2 at full blast on the car stereo and then gone to sleep.

I am not remotely comforted by the fact that the three lanes of the M25 in the other direction are not moving either, nor by the fact that the carphone rings so the helpmeet can tell me to look out for bad traffic jams on the M25.

Do not think for one minute that the carphone is part of the Houseworm's standard issue. It was acquired so that the TV presenter could call the studio and let them know she was stuck in traffic or something, and then when she got an upgrade, I got the cast off. It's known as the 10 per cent phone. Ten per cent of the time it doesn't work at all. Another 10 per cent of the time you can hear them but they can't hear you. Another 10 per cent of the time they can hear you but not you them. Another 10 per cent of the time you can both hear two other people on two other phones. Another 10 per cent of the time you get cut off in the middle. Another 10 per cent of the time you get an incomprehensible series of beeps and whistles. Another 10 per cent of the time you get the recorded voice of some toffee-nosed bint telling you the phone you have called may be switched off when you know damn well it's not. Another 10 per cent of the time the system is engaged. Another 10 per cent of the time you get radio-fade and the remaining 10 per cent of the time you don't want to make a phone call anyway.

The conclusive proof that the 'Squidgy tapes' were some Fleet Street fabrication was that at least one of the people concerned was supposed to have been talking and listening continuously, for a period of time exceeding one minute twelve seconds, on a mobile phone. Everybody knows this has never been done. Likewise Camillagate. I rest my case.

The reason wimmin get so cross with men being in charge of things like childbirth in hospitals or motorway design is that the buggers haven't got a clue what's needed from the consumer's point of view. What's needed on all roads, as any Houseworm could tell you, are public lavatories, children for the use of, every 15 feet. P.J. O'Rourke once wrote a *magnum opus* rejoicing in the title *How to Drive Fast on Drugs While Getting Your Whing-Whang Squeezed and Not Spill Your Drink*. He doesn't know the half of it. The alternative to the 'every-15-feet public lavatory' involves trying to supervise an infant piddling into a potty while driving at 70 miles an hour and simultaneously keeping everyone's seat belt on and then having to empty the bloody thing out of the window without letting the highway patrolman get a face-full. Don't tell me about splash-back, and anyway none of this bears thinking about in a dead-stopped traffic jam. So what you get is bladder-whinge for 50 miles and wet-trouser-whinge for 30.

By the time we get there the weather has begun to look like Christmas in earnest: howling gale, pouring rain and the wife's been sitting in front of the fire with a cup of tea in her greasy mitt for the last twenty minutes.

I extract the number-one son from in front of ITV's Yuletide cheer to help unload the car ('Hey, man. Like it's RAINING, y'know?'), and once that's done and I'm heading for my brother-in-law's malt Scotch to start Christmas in earnest, my sister appears and recommends that until I've boned the turkey, don't I think I'd better stick to tea, a cup of which, by an amazing coincidence, she has clutched in the hand that is not holding a 6-inch boning-knife in a suggestive manner.

Now boning turkeys is not my thing. I may be able to do it (given a sharp knife and about two and a half hours), but the fact that I could, probably, bungee jump off the Clifton Suspension Bridge does not seem to me to be a reason for setting off down the M4 equipped with a large rubber band.

Nevertheless, my wonderful sister has the following vision of Christmas: about twenty-four people, all family or extended family or waifs and strays that might otherwise not get the Dickensian delights she has planned, spend about four days in baronial splendour consuming inordinate quantities of the most wonderful food and drink available and cramming carol singing, nativity plays, party games, charades, long country walks, horse-riding and family feuds into the extraordinarily short intervals between meals.

There are remarkably few feuds, actually, mostly because there isn't time, and even mild irritation or a gloomy look gets you referred to as 'Christmassy' (*see under* 'Austria').

It's what I get when I'm boning the turkey, and my brother-in-law, whose whisky I ought to be drinking, wanders into the kitchen, picks up the tea towel I'm using, and says, 'This shouldn't be here you know . . . tea towels live over here in this drawer,' and puts it away. He is clearly unaware that I have a boning-knife in my hand.

While I am doing this, every single guest dumb enough to have uttered the words 'Can I help?' has found out that not only can they, but their respective tasks have already been allocated on the list stuck to the fridge alongside the Christmas Planner that Prue writes for the *Sunday Express* every year and then follows herself, but with a few added refinements.

One year I was also down as 'Master of the Horse'. This meant 'groom' and involved quite serious amounts of mucking out, but the upside was that after Christmas lunch I got to ride out while everybody ELSE washed-up.

Another reason for Yuletide peace prevailing among the usually egomaniacal members of our clan is that the sister's ability to plan, delegate and cook means that we're all too busy working, or finding out what our next job is, or we've got our mouths full.

Back to Yuletide preparations.

To the exhausted astonishment of all concerned, except Prue, by the time I've done the turkey and stuffed it with ham and forcemeat so that when it has to be carved I can just slice it like bread, the tree's been decorated, the table laid for the morn, the wine brought up from the cellar, the gravel swept, the flowers arranged, and the Househead has come downstairs to tell me my daughter wants a word. I go upstairs to find Rosie looking somewhat less than gruntled.

'Joe says there's no Father Christmas, it's just you and Mummy . . .'

And Happy Christmas to you too, pal.

'Of COURSE there's Father Christmas . . . where do you think PRESENTS come from? And haven't you written your letter to him? And aren't you expecting a crochet kit?'

This is all meant to distract my favourite daughter with visions of goodies to come, but to my consternation her bottom lip now crumples completely and she emits a wail a banshee could be proud of.

'I know, but now we've come to Prue's house AND HOW WILL HE KNOW WHERE WE ARE AND MY CROCHET WILL BE AT *OUR* HOUSE AND WAAAAAHHHHHH!!' This, as you might imagine, takes a little time to sort out, after which we have to POST the Father Christmas letter up the chimney, while the assembled adults try to muffle Joe's cries of, 'Why doesn't the paper just burn? And I bet it lands in the garden all covered in smoke! And how can Father Christmas read all those letters and get round all the houses in six HOURS? IT'S RIDICULOUS!'

And then we enlist him as co-conspirator and get HIM to write the note to Father Christmas that goes by the fireplace in the hall where no fire is lit ('BET HE GETS THE WRONG CHIMNEY AND BURNS HIS BUM,' Joe confides to Rosie, which has the miraculous effect of simultaneously restoring her good humour and her faith in the existence of S. Claus). Then she gets to set out the glass of milk (it used to be port, but Joe pointed out two years ago that we were encouraging drink-driving) and the mince pie which will refresh good ol' Santa, and THEN they hang up their stockings and THEN they get shooed back upstairs to bed and THEN the Houseworm gets a drink. One sip and there's a cry from the landing. I dash out, muttering death threats, to find the daughter wide-eyed and beaming at the top of the stairs. 'Is it morning?'

Nevertheless, despite these alarums and excursions, by around nine-thirty, all but the youngest houseguests are hosing down the festive cheer and stuffing their faces with smoked salmon sarnies, and the chief delegator is a picture of one who has looked upon her work and found it good.

And if you don't know how she does it, I do.

I can't do it myself, mind you.

Every other year they come to us, and while I enjoy exactly the same enthusiasm for large family Christmases that she does, my goals are slightly less ambitious (oh, all right, I DO bone the turkey; but that's from force of habit), and somehow my guests know perfectly well what an innocent 'Can I help?' is likely to get them. After all, they were at Prue's house last year.

But one year I'm going to show her up. I'm going to do the whole Trimalchio's feast bit. The turkey will not only be boned, but inside it will be a boned goose inside which will be a boned chicken inside which will be a boned duck and so on right down to the quail in the middle. And then it will all fall apart in the cooking and we'll have STEW.

By midnight of this particular Christmas Eve the decibel count is such that no-one could possibly consider that a good time is not being had by all. The Houseworm has even remembered to check up on the now angelic (because unconscious) children, and is just refreshing his glass for what may very well be the last time before joining them, when a sisterly shriek causes a sudden hush.

'Oh Gawd, we haven't done the stockings!'

I know who 'we' means, and she and I spend the next hour or so transferring the contents of her carefully prepared and labelled, quite large plastic bags into equally well-labelled quite small stockings (one for EVERY PERSON), remembering always to start with a tangerine wrapped in foil. The lateness of the hour and the natural confusion caused by very good Scotch on top of very good champagne means that this is sometimes forgotten, but the perfectionist in charge will have none of my attempts to add it in, unwrapped, later. This means a certain amount of unpacking in the name of tradition and the likely onset of Houseworm humour failure. Eventually, stockings done, I agree to write Father Christmas's note in reply to our generous hospitality and go up to bed. Tomorrow looks like being a long day.

At 3 a.m., getting up with a mouth like a Bombay burial ground, I realize that I have omitted to write said note and stagger off downstairs to do this and take a Santa Claus-type bite out of the mince pie and a slurp of milk, which, as it happens, holds some appeal. I am hoping it's still cold.

Whether it is or not, I never get to find out since my entrance into the gloom of the hall is greeted by the worst explosion of sound I have ever heard in my life. I think World War Three must have started and am about to take cover beneath the table when I realize that forgetting Father Christmas's note was pretty small beer compared with forgetting the burglar alarm.

Within two seconds every adult guest is assembled on the landing while I, dressed as I am in a pair of tartan underpants, watch my brother-in-law disarm the alarm and phone the Old Bill to put off the arrival of Gloucestershire's finest to another day. For some reason he does not appear to be speaking to me, or maybe I'm just deafened by the alarm. I write a note, take a bite of mince pie, drain the milk glass, apologize a lot more, and go back to bed. Our children have not even shifted in their sleep.

Thirty seconds later Rosie shrieks 'HAPPY CHRISTMAS!' in my ear, gets out of bed to make sure her brother's awake, and says, 'CAN WE GO AND GET OUR STOCKINGS NOW?' The clock says 5.05 a.m.

By 6.05 a.m. we have opened all the small children's presents and by 8.05 we have played all the games, done all the puzzles, tidied the room, showered, dressed in our best, and the Househead and I are taking turns at trying to get back to sleep. The one whose turn it isn't is in charge of preventing Joe from using his new bicycle siren, an item supplied, typically, by UT, the sound of which bears a remarkable resemblance to the burglar alarm and which would no doubt have precisely the same galvanizing effect on the household, only this time without the boys in blue.

Breakfast is a pretty catch-as-catch-can affair on account of having to get on with lunch. With a turkey this size, my sister ought to have been grateful for my midnight alarm, as it might well have reminded her to get the bird in the oven in time for it to cook slightly more than pale pink by lunch-time.

Another thing. Christmas is great for carnivores but the traditionalists set up the whole deal quite some time before vegetarians started to argue that the birds of the air and the beasts of the field were not necessarily put on this earth specifically so that people like my sister and Albert Roux could cook them.

The mince pies and the Christmas pud are OK, because everyone can eat veggie ones, but you try'n come up with the vegetarian equivalent of smoked salmon, turkey, ham or chipolatas. I usually settle for quails' eggs, chestnut loaf en brioche, mushroom pierogi and Glamorgan sausages. The only problem with this is that on every occasion, at least half of the carnivores say, 'Gosh, what wonderfully original ideas,' and scoff the lot.

Considering the preparation of each of these culinary triumphs takes almost twice as long as boning, stuffing and cooking a turkey, and that veggies can't pig out on OUR grub, I'm left having to stick 'HANDS OFF' notices on half the Christmas dinner.

What the pro-Dickens Christmas faction don't seem to understand is that Christmas according to Pickwick requires an army of trained servants including cook, butler, house-keeper and 'tween-stairs maid. For some inexplicable reason my sister gets to be cook, my wife and mother get to wash-up, and the Houseworm gets the rest. Christmas morning can be quite exciting what with one thing and another. On one occasion I was confident enough to report for duty wearing what even a blind man would have recognized as being one of those sweaters that are only produced in order that wives may give them to husbands for Christmas.

I had not reckoned on my sister's latest wheeze for cooking (and simultaneously shelling) chestnuts. Not for her the slitting of each individual skin followed by the slow and traditional roasting. Much quicker and simpler, thought she, to chuck 'em in a deep fat fryer turned up to max. Unfortunately this ground-breaking innovation so entranced her that she omitted the shell-slitting stage completely. At first the chestnuts simply sat in the deep oil considering their next move, which, when it came, coincided with the Houseworm's reporting for duty in his Christmas-morning woolly jumper.

They exploded. Not all at once, you understand, but each as the whim took it, like some Brobdingnagian popcorn. Each individual explosion shot boiling oil across the kitchen and prevented anyone (me, especially) getting close enough to turn off the fryer, and drops of blazing oil, ignited by the adjacent gas ring, were giving Christmas morning something of the look of Guy Fawkes night held indoors. None of this was doing my Christmas present any good at all. Finally her professional training took over and our hostess managed to fling a fire-blanket (how many people have one of THOSE in their kitchen?) over the witches' cauldron and turn off the power.

Prue looked around at her personal re-creation of the oilfields of Kuwait after Iraq came calling, and idly snuffed out a small pool of flaming oil. 'I was only doing them to try and make the brussels sprouts less disgusting than they always are. Now at least we can chuck the whole lot out. That sweater looks a bit greasy. Hurry up and change, we're getting behind schedule.'

By the time we were back on schedule, around 2 p.m., and ready to go, we had already dealt with stockings from around the chimney breast, inter-familial presents with morning coffee and mince pies, which had been preceded by church for those for whom the Almighty represented a more pressing call on their time than turkey-basting and wine-opening. I was not among their number.

Trying to cook TWO Christmas dinners, one vegetarian, even in a kitchen as well equipped as that belonging to the author of the *Cookery Bible*, means that at the last minute you run out of oven space at almost exactly the same moment as the oven runs out of heat. Amusingly, this astonishing coincidence is invariably compounded by the fact that the LPG cylinder that powers the gas rings chooses this precise moment to declare itself empty. Its replacement, if we WANT gravy, will need to be fetched from the garage by guess who. Since this thing weighs approximately 50 kilos, by the time it's been lifted out, trolleyed in, man-handled into position and connected up, I need to shower and change all over again.

These logistical problems occur with such frequency that my niece has the unenviable task of ensuring that each portion of nutmeat brioche finds its way to the festive board via a quick forty-five seconds in the microwave. In any event, by the time twenty odd revellers, by now fizzing with pre-lunch champagne, have been persuaded to sit down, the turkey and brioche have been presented and applauded, the carving has been done, the vegetables dished up and the wine poured and the hostess and the home help have finally sat down and said, 'pass the bread sauce', just about everything is lukewarm. There is no way around this, short of heating up the plates to the point at which younger celebrants spend New Year in the burns unit of the John Radcliffe.

Every year I vow to start a movement for the abolition of the traditional Christmas menu, totally unsuited as it is to the service of large numbers of people who are already more full of mince pies than they ought to be, and its replacement by a large fish pie, topped with cheesy mashed potato and served with a green salad. The pie will keep hot for ever, taste sensational and you can serve cold roast turkey and cold ham as a buffet on Boxing Day. Remember you read it here first.

The day after Boxing Day finds the Houseworm and his family, to the unutterable relief of his brother-in-law and erstwhile host, heading back down the A34 for home. As he drives, he wonders how it is that the getting and giving of presents never, ever results in a net gain of space in the car. The only difference in the driver's discomfort on the return trip is that the handlebars sticking in his ear now have a siren attached. And not even Joe's enthusiasm for suddenly setting it off 'as a joke, OK?' can keep the Houseworm from the consideration of what domestic disasters might await him at home, knowing, as he does, that although the year might be over, and the Prime Ministerial biography written, once you have been a Houseworm there is no going back.

Will the washing-machine be bleating its idiotic cry of distress? Will the central heating have broken down? Or will the drains have backed up again?

But that is where you came in.

February 1994.

Acknowledgements

MANY THANKS TO MY AGENT, JANE TURNBULL, WHO LIKED the idea, and to Sally Gaminara and all at Doubleday who agreed with her.

Further thanks are due to The John Lewis Partnership for providing the pinstripe suit on the cover which so signally fails to conceal the Houseworm within.

The original impetus for this book came from the strong desire I felt to go back to university to study psychology, in order at least to try to understand the incomprehensible (to me at least) reactions and attitudes of my fellow men and women to my new occupation.

I made a start by speaking to Professor Cary Cooper of UMIST, and Angela J. Thompson.

On their advice I read several books on 'role reversal' and

then spent several weeks on the many books and articles on 'The Sex War' that seemed so popular in the early Nineties.

My reading included *Career Couples* by Professor Cooper with Suzanne Lewis, Neil Lyndon's *No More Sex War*, Yvonne Roberts' *Mad about Women*, Mary Miedzian's *Boys will be Boys* and Robert Bly's *Iron John*.

I am deeply grateful to all these writers, together with Germaine Greer, David Thomas, Andrea Dworkin, Betty Friedan and Gloria Steinem who together convinced me that the only people qualified to discuss the psychology of role reversal and the rights, wrongs and responsibilities of The Sex War, are those who do NOT have four children, a house, assorted pets and a working partner to get through the day.

Those of us who DO, simply don't have the time.